Thailand

Thailand

BY MEL FRIEDMAN

Enchantment of the World™
Second Series

CHILDREN'S PRESS®

An Imprint of Scholastic Inc.

New York   Toronto   London   Auckland   Sydney
Mexico City   New Delhi   Hong Kong
Danbury, Connecticut

Frontispiece: **Boats, Phi Phi Islands**

Consultant: Kennon Breazeale, PhD, Projects Coordinator, Research Program, East-West Center, Honolulu, Hawaii
Please note: All statistics are as up-to-date as possible at the time of publication.

Book production by The Design Lab

Library of Congress Cataloging-in-Publication Data
Friedman, Mel, 1946–
  Thailand / by Mel Friedman.
     pages cm. — (Enchantment of the world. Second series)
  Includes bibliographical references and index.
  ISBN 978-0-531-20791-8 (lib. bdg.)
  1. Thailand—Juvenile literature. I. Title.
  DS563.5.F753 2015
  959.3—dc23   2014001867

1 2 3 4 5 6 7 8 9 10 R 24 23 22 21 20 19 18 17 16 15

Floating market

Contents

Left to right: **Floating market, wai, family, planting rice, floating lanterns**

CHAPTER 1

Land of Beauty, Land of Grace

THE COUNTRY OF THAILAND IS BLESSED WITH A LUSH climate, abundant natural resources, and a glorious history and culture that stretch back thousands of years. Thailand is located in the center of Southeast Asia. It is a stunningly beautiful land that naturally divides into four geographic regions. Journey from one region to another and you enter a different world, each with its own landscape and customs. Its geography varies from towering mountains to fertile valleys to warm blue seas.

In Thailand's art, architecture, and archaeological sites, it is possible to glimpse the magnificence of its ancient civilizations. Thailand is also a country that has enthusiastically embraced the new. Over the past few decades, its economy has been rapidly industrializing, and its cities—especially its capital, Bangkok—pulse with youthful energy and excitement.

Opposite: **Bells hang at Wat Saket, the Temple of the Golden Mountain, in Bangkok.**

THAILAND

- ● Cities of more than 140,000 people
- ○ Other cities
- ✪ National capital

0   200 miles
0   200 kilometers

MYANMAR (BURMA)

LAOS

South China Sea

Chiang Rai
Doi Luang National Park
Phayao
Chiang Mai
Nan
Lampang
Phrae
Uttaradit
Loei
Nong Khai
Nakhon Phanom
Tak
Sukhothai
Udon Thani
Nam Nao National Park
Phu Phon National Park
Phichit
Khon Kaen
Mukdahan
Kamphaeng Phet
Nakhon Sawan
Chaiyaphum
Ubon Ratchathani
Chainat
Nakhon Ratchasima
Buriram
Surin
Khaoen Si Nakarin National Park
Sara Buri
Khao Yai National Park
Thap Lan National Park
Phu Chong Nayoi Nat'l Park
Erawan National Park
Ayutthaya
Pak Kret
Pang Sida National Park
Nonthaburi
Bangkok
Samut Prakan
Chon Buri
CAMBODIA
Kaeng Krachan Nat'l Park
Phetchaburi
Pattaya
Hua Hin
Rayong
Chanthaburi
Trat
Mu Ko Chang Marine Nat'l Park
VIETNAM
Prachuap Khiri Khan
Bang Saphan Yai

Andaman Sea

Chumphon
Ranong
Gulf of Thailand

Khao Sok National Park
Surat Thani
Tai Rom Yen National Park
Takua Pa
Phangnga
Nakhon Si Thammarat
Krabi
Phuket
Trang
Songkhla
Hat Yai
Pattani
Satun
Yala
Tarutao National Park
Narathiwat

INDONESIA

MALAYSIA

Thailand

    The Thai people are proud of their heritage. For eight hundred years, they have fought off and driven back every invading nation that tried to conquer their land. In fact, Thailand is the only country in Southeast Asia never colonized by Europeans. The Thai name of the country, *Prathet Thai*, boldly trumpets this fact. The word *Thai* means "free." *Prathet Thai* means "Thailand," but it also can be translated as "Land of the Free."

Thailand has been a constitutional monarchy since 1932. Its government is democratically elected, but its head of state is a king. Democracy has had a troubled history in the country. Periodically, the powerful Thai military has stepped in to overthrow governments and install leaders it preferred. In May 2014, the military seized control of the government to end months of violent clashes between members of the two main political parties.

A woman holds up a picture of King Bhumibol Adulyadej before he gives a speech. He has been king since 1946.

Symbol of a Nation

A mythical creature called Garuda often serves as a national symbol for Thailand. Garuda is a creature that appears in classical Hindu religious tales. It has the head, beak, wings, and talons of an eagle and the body of a man. On its head sits a crown. In Indian literature, Garuda fights evil and carries the Hindu god Vishnu across the earth. Garuda was said to be so big that its wings blotted out the sun. When the king of Thailand honors a company for its good deeds, he permits it to use Garuda's image as a royal seal of approval.

The overwhelming majority of Thai people speak the same language (Thai) and share the same religious heritage,

Buddhist monks walk up stairs at a temple in Bangkok.

Buddhism. Over the centuries, Buddhism has been the most significant influence on Thai art, architecture, music, culture, and ways of life. From Buddhism, Thais have learned to avoid conflict and practice tolerance, patience, and compromise. They have also developed a sense of playfulness and an easy-going approach toward life.

Thais call this easygoing attitude *sanuk*. *Sanuk* is often translated as "fun," but it means much more than that. To enjoy every moment to its fullest is sanuk, and to be able to look on the bright side even if things don't go your way is also sanuk. For Thais, a life without sanuk would be too dreary to imagine. If you visit Thailand one day, you will be able to experience the kindness and graciousness of the Thai people. You will also get to see the beautiful cultural treasures of one of the world's great civilizations.

Thailand is filled with bustling markets where shoppers can buy a wide variety of foods.

CHAPTER 2

The Jewel of Southeast Asia

THAILAND IS A LAND OF REMARKABLE BEAUTY LOCATED in the heart of mainland Southeast Asia. It covers an area of 198,117 square miles (513,120 square kilometers), which is larger than California but smaller than Texas. Its 3,022-mile (4,863-kilometer) border touches four countries: Myanmar (formerly Burma) to the north and west, Laos to the north and east, Cambodia to the southeast, and Malaysia to the south. Given its central location in Southeast Asia, Thailand has served for centuries as a crossroads—and sometimes a battleground—for different Asian peoples, cultures, and religious traditions.

Opposite: **Flowers carpet a hillside at the foot of Doi Inthanon, the tallest mountain in Thailand.**

A Tale of Four Regions

Thais traditionally compare the shape of their country to the shape of an elephant's head, with each part of the head corresponding to a different geographical region. The top of the head is the north; the big ear, the northeast; the mouth, the central region; and the long dangling trunk, the south.

Thailand's Geographic Features

Area: 198,117 square miles (513,120 sq km)

Length of Coastline: About 2,000 miles (3,200 km)

Highest Elevation: Doi Inthanon, 8,481 feet (2,585 m)

Lowest Elevation: Sea level, along the coast

Principal River: Chao Phraya River, about 225 miles (365 km)

Longest River: Chi River, about 475 miles (765 km)

Largest Lake: Songkhla, on the Malay Peninsula, about 402 square miles (1,041 sq km)

Wettest Region: Malay Peninsula, about 150 inches (380 cm) of rain annually

Driest Region: Northeast, about 40 inches (100 cm) of rain annually

Average Annual High Temperature: 100°F (38°C)

Average Annual Low Temperature: about 66°F (19°C)

Northern Thailand is a mountainous area with narrow river valleys in which fruits such as oranges, apples, tomatoes, strawberries, and lychees are grown. Doi Inthanon, located in the Thanon Thong Chai Mountain Range that lies along Thailand's northwestern border with Myanmar, is the country's highest peak, at 8,481 feet (2,585 meters). Farther north is the Tanen Range, which stretches like a roadblock across Thailand's upper frontier with Myanmar; while the Luang Prabang Range to the east parallels a lengthy section of the Thai-Laotian border. Four major rivers—the Ping, Wang, Yom, and Nan—begin in these highlands. From there, they flow southward until they converge to form the great Chao Phraya River, which has nourished Thailand's agricultural heartland for generations. Apart from the historic city of Chiang Mai, the cultural capital of the north, the region is sparsely populated.

Until about the mid-twentieth century, the mountains of the north were carpeted with hardwood forests. Since then, the woodlands have been destroyed. They have been logged

The Mekong is the longest river in Southeast Asia. It marks the border between Thailand and Laos in two different places.

and burned to create farm fields. In 1989, the government took important steps toward ending illegal logging. Yet, preserving what remains of Thailand's precious old-growth forests still represents one of the country's greatest environmental challenges.

The northeast region, known as Isan, is a vast flatland with nutrient-poor soil. The region is prone to flooding in the rainy season and drought in the dry season. It receives the least amount of rainfall of any Thai region, and farming there is limited to hardy crops. These include cassava, corn, tapioca, cotton, and mulberry trees (the leaves of which are used in silk production).

The dominant geographical feature of Isan is the vast Khorat Plateau. The Mun and Chi Rivers cut across the plateau like sashes. The Mekong River, which defines a large part of the Thai-Laotian border, forms the plateau's northern and eastern edges. On the west and south, the plateau is bordered by the

Phetchabun and the Dangrek Ranges. The Dangrek range separates Thailand from Cambodia. The people of Isan share many traditions with the neighboring peoples of Laos and Cambodia.

Thailand's central plain is one of the finest rice-producing regions in the world. Flooding in this region has traditionally worked to the farmer's advantage. The land in the region, unlike that in Isan, is continually replenished with rich deposits of soil and sediment carried down from the northern mountains by the Chao Phraya River and its tributaries. An intricate network of irrigation canals crisscrosses the region, enabling many rice farmers to have three harvests a year. Mountains and

Rice requires a lot of water to flourish and is often grown in flooded fields.

plateaus flank the central plain on the west, north, and east. In the south, the plain borders the Gulf of Thailand.

The central plain is the cultural, economic, and political heartland of Thailand. Three cities in this region—Ayutthaya, Thonburi, and Bangkok—have served as capitals of successive Thai kingdoms. About one-third of all Thais now live in the central plain, making it the most densely populated region of the country.

Southern Thailand lies along a mountainous strip of land called the Malay Peninsula. Mainland Asia is connected to the Malay Peninsula by the Isthmus of Kra, which is only about

People come from all over the world to enjoy the beautiful beaches and towering rock formations of Phuket.

27 miles (44 kilometers) at its narrowest. Thailand shares this peninsula with two other countries: Myanmar to the west and Malaysia to the south. The border here with Myanmar is defined by the Bilauktaung Range, which winds down the peninsula like a crooked spine. Its peaks rise as high as 7,000 feet (2,100 m). South of this range and the Isthmus of Kra, Thailand widens until it touches the seas on both sides: the Gulf of Thailand in the east and the Andaman Sea in the west.

Phuket is a teardrop-shaped island in the Andaman Sea off the west coast of southern Thailand. The island, which was settled as early as the first century BCE, is noted for its beautiful beaches and stunning rock formations. It is one of Thailand's top tourist destinations.

The south receives the heaviest amount of rainfall in Thailand, about 150 inches (380 centimeters) per year. Rice and oil palms, which produce an oil used in cooking, are farmed there. Other economic activities include tin and gemstone mining and fishing.

Hot and Wet

Thailand is a tropical country that has three distinct seasons: rainy, cool, and hot. Changes in seasons are governed by monsoons, winds that reverse direction in response to seasonal variations between land and sea temperatures.

In about May or June, moisture-laden ocean winds begin blowing inland from the southwest, signaling the start of Thailand's rainy season. This monsoon lasts at least through September and dumps an average of 60 inches (150 cm) of rain

Urban Explosion

Thailand is undergoing dramatic urban growth. Since 1997, the number of municipalities that the government officially classifies as *nakhons*, or "cities," has more than tripled. The capital city of Bangkok, with a population of about 8.3 million, still eclipses all other Thai cities in size and power, but many other cities are growing rapidly.

Nonthaburi (right), a suburb of Bangkok, is Thailand's second-largest city and the capital of Nonthaburi Province. With nearly 300,000 residents, it is one of the fastest-growing cities in the central region. Its location near the mouth of the Chao Phraya River makes it an important hub for trade and commerce. Thailand's third-largest city, Pak Kret, has a population of nearly 200,000 and is also a suburb of Bangkok.

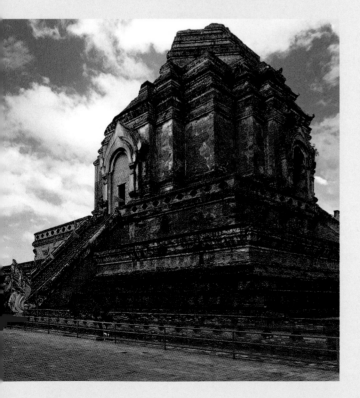

Hat Yai is the largest city in the south, with a population of about 160,000. It has a high proportion of ethnic Malay and Chinese residents. The gateway to the northeast, Nakhon Ratchasima, is an industrial city with a population of a little over 140,000. Archaeological digs not far from the city have uncovered evidence of human settlements on the Khorat Plateau dating back four thousand years.

Chiang Mai is the largest city in the mountainous north. A little more than 140,000 people live in Chiang Mai, which sits some 1,000 feet (300 m) above sea level along the Ping River, a major tributary of the Chao Phraya River. Towering above it is Doi Suthep, one of Thailand's tallest mountains. The city is home to more than three hundred Buddhist temples (left). The oldest, Wat Chiang Man, was built in the thirteenth century. Chiang Mai's relatively cool tropical climate is ideal for raising flowers, including prized varieties of orchids. The city holds a flower festival every February.

on the land. The heaviest amount of rain falls on the Isthmus of Kra. Countrywide temperatures during the rainy season average about 84 degrees Fahrenheit (29 degrees Celsius).

In October or November, the rainfall tapers off as the monsoon reverses direction. Now, the prevailing winds blow seaward from the northeast, bearing drier weather. During the dry season, the average amount of rainfall in Thailand is just 6 to 10 inches (15 to 25 cm), and temperatures range from about 82°F to 90°F (28°C to 32°C). Southern Thailand has the shortest dry season; the northeast has the longest.

In February, the dry season gives way to a three-month transitional period in which temperatures climb and the prevailing winds swing around to blow once more from the southeast. During this time, Thailand swelters under its hottest weather. Temperatures in March and April, for example, routinely top 100°F (38°C).

Rain pours down on Bangkok most afternoons during the rainy season, from May to October.

The Day the Ocean Floor Shook

On December 26, 2004, a powerful earthquake rocked the ocean floor off the northwest coast of Indonesia, unleashing a deadly tsunami. A tsunami is a giant surface wave or series of waves that is sometimes generated by a violent undersea event. A tsunami can rip across the ocean surface, almost unnoticed, at speeds of up to 500 miles per hour (800 kph). As it approaches the shallower depths near shore, the wave rears up to form a towering wall of water up to 100 feet (30 m) high.

The 2004 tsunami was one of the worst natural disasters in history, and the worst disaster ever to hit Thailand. It struck thirteen countries around the Indian Ocean and Andaman Sea, killing approximately 200,000 people, including 8,000 in Thailand. Many hundreds of thousands more went missing. Significant parts of Thailand's west coast and islands were damaged. More than 150,000 Thais working in the fishing or tourist industries lost their livelihoods.

By mid-2005, Thailand had activated its first tsunami early-warning system. The system quickly proved its worth when thousands of people on the Malay Peninsula were safely evacuated in response to a tsunami alarm. Thailand was lucky that time, because a devastating tsunami did not arrive.

Conserving Natural Treasures

The forests of Thailand are great national treasures. Unfortunately, Thailand has had the second-highest rate of forest loss in Southeast Asia, exceeded only by Singapore's. In 1960, forests covered more than half of Thailand. Today, only about one-quarter of the country remains wooded, because of unchecked logging and clear-cutting to carve out new farmland.

Deforestation can have catastrophic consequences. The roots of trees hold soil in place, preventing erosion. Thailand's forests teem with wildlife and sustain countless plant species. With the loss of their habitats, many native animal and plant species in Thailand are now threatened with extinction.

Damage to the environment has also contributed to the frequency of certain natural disasters. When woodlands are stripped bare, the soil does not retain water. Instead, it washes easily down hillsides during rainstorms, sometimes in torrential floods or landslides. One of the country's worst landslides occurred in southern Thailand in November 1988. Hundreds

When all the plant life is stripped from hillsides, erosion and mudslides become more common.

of people were injured or killed. In the autumn of 2011, the country suffered its worst flooding in seventy years. More than one thousand factories closed and more than eight hundred people died.

A few years prior to the 1988 landslide, the government had begun to address the gravity of Thailand's environmental crisis. It set aside one-quarter of Thailand as protected forests. In 1989, the Thai government banned all commercial logging. Three other laws were added to this landmark law in 1992,

Thais wade and boat through the streets of Nonthaburi in 2011. The flooding affected millions of Thais.

calling for reforesting woodlands, conserving the environment, and safeguarding wildlife. Today, Thailand gets much of its wood from neighboring countries.

Trails lead through the thick forests at Khao Yai National Park.

Expanding National Parks

As part of its effort to protect the environment, Thailand has been expanding its national park system. It now has more than one hundred national parks, including twenty-one marine national parks. Three dozen new national and marine parks are currently being developed. Today, Thailand's national park system accounts for roughly 14 percent of the country's total land area. Khao Yai National Park, at the southwestern boundary of the Khorat Plateau, is Thailand's oldest national park, established in 1961. Kaeng Krachan National Park, located toward the top of the Malay Peninsula, is currently its largest.

CHAPTER 3

Nature's Bounty

THAILAND'S TROPICAL CLIMATE AND VARYING geography create rich ecosystems for supporting life. In this relatively small country live more than 15,000 varieties of plants and 16,000 species of animals, nearly 10 percent of all animal species on earth. The country is home to 285 different types of mammals, 960 nonmigratory bird species, 1,900 fish species, 310 reptile species, and 107 amphibian species. Thailand is also home to thousands of kinds of insects, including 1,200 types of butterflies.

Forests of the North

Many animals make their home in the Thai forest. Two different types of forests flourish in the northern, northeastern, and central regions: monsoon and savanna. Monsoon forests, found in the mountains, are densely wooded. Their thick, leafy trees provide shelter and camouflage for animals of all sizes. During the dry season, most of these trees shed their

Orchids

Orchids are exquisite flowers that come in many different sizes, shapes, and colors. Although orchids look delicate, they are actually very hardy plants. They can grow on trees, in the ground, between rocks, and at almost any altitude. Orchids are also able to tolerate dry climates well. They thrive as easily in Thailand's arid northeastern plateau as they do in its wet southern rain forests. All told, some 1,500 orchid species grow in Thailand, and in recent years, the country has emerged as the world's leading exporter of tropical orchids.

leaves. Teak, bamboo, and other hardwoods flourish in these northern forests, as do many beautiful varieties of orchids, Thailand's most famous flower.

Most of Thailand's monsoon forests are now protected in national parks and wildlife sanctuaries. Among the many animal species living in these preserves are elephants, tigers, bears, leopards, gibbons, gaurs (wild oxen), macaques (short-

National Tree: Golden Shower Tree

The ratchaphruek, or golden shower tree, is Thailand's national tree. The tree ranges in height from 35 to 70 feet (11 to 21 m). It has oval leaves and produces clusters of bright yellow flowers. The golden shower tree plays an important role in traditional medicine in Thailand, with different parts of the tree being used to treat everything from burns to fevers to coughs. Its bloom is Thailand's national flower.

tailed monkeys), wild pigs, muntjacs and sambars (types of deer), dholes (wild dogs), and hundreds of kinds of birds.

Savanna forests are grasslands dotted with shrubs and trees. Sometimes these forests develop as a result of soil and climatic conditions. More commonly, they replace thickly wooded forests that have been damaged or destroyed by fire or logging. That is why many of Thailand's savanna forests lie at the boundaries of its monsoon forests. Asian elephants, Asiatic water buffalo, pygmy hogs, and tigers are all found in savanna forests.

Water buffalo spend a great deal of time in the water, which helps them cool off in hot climates.

National Animal: Asian Elephant

Beloved for their gentle nature and innate intelligence, elephants are symbols of majesty and power in Thailand. They also occupy a special place in the Hindu and Buddhist traditions that are the wellsprings of religious faith in Thailand. For centuries, elephants were used for transportation, to do heavy work, and to help in warfare. In the sixteenth century, Thai troops mounted on elephants defeated an invading force from neighboring Burma. Thais believe that they owe the very freedom of their country to the bravery of this elephant cavalry. The former national flag of Thailand depicted a white elephant on a red background.

Asian elephants are different from their African cousins. Asian elephants are distinguished by their pointy ears and smaller size. "Smaller," of course, is relative. Thai elephants are still among the largest animals in the world. They range in height from 6.5 feet (2 m) to 11.5 feet (3.5 m), and weigh around 11,000 pounds (5,000 kilograms). From trunk to tail, they measure about 21 feet (6.4 m). All elephants are plant-eaters. The daily diet of an elephant consists of as much as 500 pounds (225 kg) of grass, leaves, fruit, and bark.

A century ago more than one hundred thousand wild elephants roamed the Thai countryside. Today, only about twenty to twenty-five thousand are alive in Thailand. Of these, very few are wild. Most reside in national parks and protected sanctuaries. Asian elephants in Thailand and elsewhere have been officially classified as an endangered species.

World's Smallest Bat

More than a hundred different kinds of bats have been identified in Thailand. One of the rarest is Kitti's hog-nosed bat, which is nicknamed the bumblebee bat. It is the smallest bat in the world, and may be the smallest mammal. It measures just a bit more than 1 inch (2.5 centimeters) long and weighs less than 0.1 ounce (3 grams). The bat is able to hover like a hummingbird, despite the fact that it has no tail to stabilize it in flight. Kitti's hog-nosed bat lives in the limestone caves of western Thailand. It leaves its roost only for about half an hour in the evening to feed on flying insects. Discovered in 1974, it is now listed as vulnerable, with only about two thousand known to exist in Thailand.

In the Rain Forest

Southern Thailand, where rainfall is most abundant, has two other forest habitats: tropical rain forests and coastal mangrove forests. This region's surviving patches of tropical rain forests lie adjacent to mountains. They are evergreen forests, meaning that their trees do not shed their leaves. Trees in the rain forest can grow as high as 270 feet (80 m). The dominant tree of the southern rain forests is a lofty hardwood named *Dipterocarpaceae*, or "two-winged fruit." Competing below for the weak sunlight that filters down through the forest canopy are palm trees, bamboos, strangler figs, climbing vines, ferns, insect-eating pitcher plants, and flowers such as *Rafflesias* (the largest flower in the world) and orchids.

Many magnificent mammals live in Thailand's rain forests, from elephants to tigers to crocodiles. Native species whose

Spectacled langur babies are bright orange. They turn gray when they are about nine months old.

dwindling numbers put them at risk include clouded leopards, gaurs (the largest species of wild ox), Malayan tapirs (a piglike animal), Malayan sun bears, binturongs (a catlike creature), Fea's muntjacs (a small deer), Dyak fruit bats, and primates such as spectacled langurs and slow lorises.

Marvelous Mangroves

Most of Thailand's mangrove forests are along the Malay coastline, near the mouths of rivers and low-lying swampy areas. Mangrove trees are unusual in that they thrive in seawater. Fish and shellfish nest and feed in their long, tangled roots. These roots extend below the water, anchoring the shore against the flux of tides and storm surges.

Mangrove roots are excellent water filters. They remove many pollutants from the water that might harm sea life. The mangrove forests help sea creatures such as dugongs (sea mammals), Irrawaddy dolphins, sea bass, barracudas, mangrove jacks (red snappers), and tree-climbing crabs and sea snails. Many birds roost in the branches of the mangrove tree, and diverse species of monkeys feast on its shoots and leaves. Over the years, farmers have cleared many irreplaceable mangrove forests to raise shrimp, cultivate rice, or plant rubber trees.

Reptiles

They slither, they crawl, they swim, they hop—and sometimes they bite. Thailand's landscape is populated with many kinds of snakes, lizards, frogs, and toads. Among Thailand's 175 species of snakes are deadly cobras, kraits, vipers, and pythons. The king cobra is native to the Malay Peninsula. Measuring up to 24 feet (7 m) long, it is the world's biggest poisonous snake. When challenged, it rears up, displays its fearsome hood, and hisses menacingly. Venom from a cobra bite can kill a person in fifteen minutes and an elephant in an hour.

The reticulated python also lives in the south. This python is among the largest snakes in the world. The record for the longest snake of this species is 33 feet (10 meters). Equipped with powerful muscles, reticulated pythons are crushers, not poisoners like cobras. After sinking their teeth into a victim, they wind their body around it, and then, quite literally, squeeze the life out of it. Chickens, ducks, rodents, and small

Reticulated pythons are the world's longest snakes.

pigs are typical prey. Some Thais, especially those living in urban areas, value pythons as rodent catchers. Only rarely do these snakes attack human beings.

Thailand boasts one of the oldest surviving reptiles on earth, the monitor lizard. Native to southern Thailand, this throwback to the age of dinosaurs is huge. Some measure as much as 7 feet (2 m) from nose to tail. Their powerful jaws and tails are lethal weapons. The bite of a monitor lizard is poisonous and can be fatal. Despite their great size, monitor lizards are good swimmers and surprisingly fleet-footed. When pursuing their prey—insects, birds, other reptiles, and small mammals—they sometimes climb up trees.

Feathered Friends

Thailand is a bird-watcher's paradise. One-tenth of all bird species in the world are native to Thailand. Hundreds of others flock there from other countries to escape winter's cold, to breed, or to rest up before resuming longer migratory flights. Many colorful mountain and forest birds find Thailand's northern climates ideal. Among these are purple swamphens, great hornbills, barbets, and green-tailed sunbirds.

A remarkable bird found in the southern peninsula is the tiny swiftlet. It builds a nest high up on cave walls from its own saliva. Unfortunately for swiftlets, their nests are the key ingredient in bird's nest soup, a Chinese delicacy. Humans harvest these nests and sell them to restaurants across Asia. Sometimes these nests have not been abandoned, and whatever eggs or live young they contain are destroyed.

A Fish Story

More than 2,500 species of saltwater and freshwater fish dwell in the waters of Southeast Asia. Off Thailand's coasts swim many saltwater game fish, including tuna, marlin, sea bass, sailfish, mackerel, mahimahi, tigerfish, and several types of sharks. Inland, about 1,100 species are native to the Mekong River region alone. This great river, which runs along the Thai-Laotian border, is the world's most productive inland fishery. One-quarter of all freshwater fish caught in the world comes from this region. Unique species such as the Irrawaddy dolphin, giant freshwater stingray, and Mekong giant catfish inhabit its waters.

Saving the Environment

In many places across Thailand, habitats and the animals that live there are in decline. The spread of Thai cities and deforestation have reduced many once-sprawling habitats to small, disconnected patches. Illegal hunting, or poaching, has also taken a severe toll on the animals. Elephants are killed for their valuable ivory. Other species, most notably tigers and rhinoceroses, have become prime targets for poachers and smugglers. The illegal and highly profitable trade in rare wildlife has been booming, in part, because of false beliefs in some countries that body parts of certain animals have great medicinal power. To safeguard its wildlife, the Thai government has established more than 180 protected areas in which animals can roam freely. These national parks, wildlife sanctuaries, and no-hunting zones collectively account for about 20 percent of Thailand's total area. The government has also stepped up its efforts to crack down on illegal trappers and smugglers. It remains to be seen whether Thailand's efforts to preserve its precious natural heritage for future generations will be successful.

The Fish That (Almost) Isn't One

The mudskipper is a small tropical fish whose odd behavior seems to defy the laws of a fish's nature. A resident of Thailand's mangrove swamps and mudflats, the mudskipper is about 6 inches (15 cm) long and has bulging eyes. When the tide goes out, exposing the shoreline, the mudskipper uses its strong fins to flap its way over the mudflats. It can move faster out of water than in it. If it keeps its skin moist and retains water in its gills, the fish can remain out of the water without suffocating for a few days. The mudskipper eats algae in tidal pools and preys on insects and small shellfish. It has even been known to slither up a mangrove tree in search of its next meal.

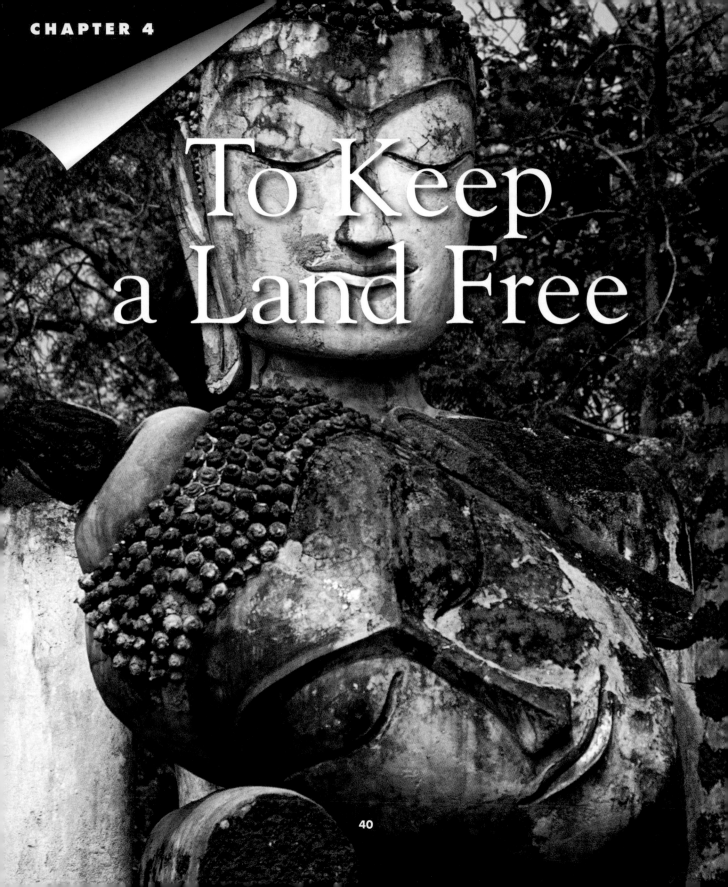

CHAPTER 4

To Keep a Land Free

PEOPLE HAVE BEEN LIVING IN WHAT IS NOW THAILAND for thousands of years. Archaeologists have unearthed evidence of settlements in the northeast that date to 3600 BCE. Evidence suggests that these early cultures were based upon farming. People planted rice, raised chickens and pigs, caught fish, and made pottery and jewelry. What happened to these ancient people is a mystery. After about 250 BCE, all traces of their civilization vanished.

Opposite: **Buddha statues at the Kamphaeng Phet Historical Park date back to the fourteenth century.**

Migrations

Over the next several centuries, a number of different groups migrated to Thailand from neighboring parts of Asia. These included groups from southern and western China. One of these peoples, known as the Mon, established several kingdoms between the sixth and ninth centuries CE in what is today southern Myanmar and west-central Thailand. Mon people have been living in these areas ever since.

The Mon were heavily influenced by close cultural and trading ties with India to the west. They became the first people in mainland Southeast Asia to adopt an Indian religion, Buddhism. The Mon, in turn, played a critical role in spreading Buddhist teachings and philosophy throughout the region. Their culture is also noted for its beautiful artwork, especially its Buddhist sculptures.

Closely related to the Mon people were the Khmer, the ancestors of modern-day Cambodians. In the ninth century, Khmer rulers founded an empire that was centered on Cambodia but eventually embraced eastern Thailand and major parts of

Examples of Khmer architecture still exist in northeastern Thailand. The ruins at Phimai date to the eleventh century.

Laos and Vietnam. The Khmer defeated the Mon in the eleventh century. Whereas Mon culture was inspired by Indian Buddhism, the Buddhism practiced by the Khmer was influenced by Indian Hinduism. Examples of Khmer temple architecture can still be seen in northeastern Thailand.

Arrival of the Thais

The Thais came later to the land that one day would bear their name. Scholars believe that the Thais were part of a much larger group of Tai-speaking peoples who, ages earlier, had relocated to southern China from their homes in northern Vietnam. The second mass migration of Thai tribes—from China to Thailand—occurred over hundreds of years, beginning in the tenth or eleventh century. Thai immigrants settled first in the northern hills. Then they gradually pushed southward into Thailand's fertile central plain. By the start of the thirteenth century, Thai settlements reached as far south as the Malay Peninsula. All these scattered Thai communities were dominated by the Mon or Khmer.

Then, in the early 1200s, Thai settlers began to rebel. A prince named Indraditya seized the Khmer city of Sukhothai in the upper Chao Phraya River valley. Other Thai principalities soon united behind him. Indraditya declared Sukhothai an

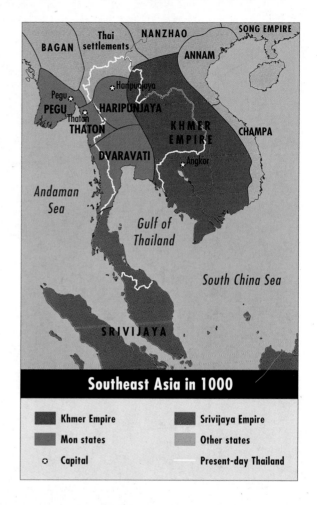

Southeast Asia in 1000

Khmer Empire
Mon states
Capital
Srivijaya Empire
Other states
Present-day Thailand

Wat Chiang Man was built in 1297. It is the oldest temple in Chiang Mai.

independent kingdom, and he became its first king. Sukhothai became a center for Theravada Buddhism, a school of teachings that was to become the dominant religion of Thailand.

Toward the end of the thirteenth century, another Thai leader, Mangrai, established a separate Thai kingdom in the north called Lan Na. At its height, Lan Na included most of northern Thailand as well as parts of Burma, Laos, and China. In 1296, Mangrai built a new capital near the Ping River for his kingdom. He named it Chiang Mai, which means "New Town." The kingdom remained independent until the sixteenth century, when it was conquered by the Burmese and incorporated into their empire.

The Dawn of Happiness

Many Thais look back upon the Sukhothai period (1238–1438) as the golden age of Thai history. Sukhothai, which means the "dawn of happiness," was the first independent Thai kingdom.

During the Sukhothai period, the people of the central valley began referring to themselves as "thai," their word for "free." They did so, it is believed, to set themselves apart from other peoples who spoke similar languages but had not yet broken away from their foreign masters. The high point of the Sukhothai period was the reign of Indraditya's second son, Ramkhamhaeng (Rama the Brave), who ruled from 1279 to 1298.

Sukhothai went into a slow decline following Ramkhamhaeng's death. Soon, an upstart kingdom in the south took over leadership of the region. It was called Ayutthaya, and its line of kings would rule Thailand for the next four hundred years.

Rama the Brave

Ramkhamhaeng (1239?–1298), whose name means "Rama the Brave," was by all accounts a fair and just ruler of Sukhothai. A deeply religious man, he did much to increase interest in the Theravada school of Buddhism. Many Buddhist temples, monasteries, and bronze statues of the Buddha were built during his rule. According to Thai tradition, Ramkhamhaeng invented the Thai alphabet by adapting elements from Khmer and Mon scripts. A stone inscription of his words, now in the Bangkok National Museum, is said to be the earliest surviving example of Thai writing. Sukhothai developed warm relations with China during Ramkhamhaeng's reign. In appreciation, the Chinese emperor had his artists and craftsmen teach Thai artisans how to make fine pottery in the Chinese way.

Ayutthaya

The city of Ayutthaya was founded in 1351 on an island in the Chao Phraya River, not far from present-day Bangkok. It was named after Ayodhya, a holy city in India.

During the Ayutthaya period, Theravada Buddhism emerged as the kingdom's chief religion. Ayutthaya rulers, adopting many Hindu and Khmer practices, demanded to be treated as living gods. They asserted absolute power over the lives of their subjects. Only family members were allowed to gaze upon a king's face or address him directly. To manage their kingdom, Ayutthaya rulers created a legal and political

Ayutthaya was one of the most powerful kingdoms in Asia. Today, all that remains of the old city are ruins.

The Hero Queen

In 1549, a Burmese army invaded the kingdom of Ayutthaya. To defend Ayutthaya, the king, Maha Chakapat, called out his foot soldiers and musketeers, rolled out his cannons, and assembled his great war elephants for battle. His beloved Queen Suriyothai begged him to let her accompany him into battle. She refused to take no for an answer, and reluctantly he agreed. Disguising herself as a man, Suriyothai mounted an elephant and rode out beside her husband.

Soon, the king sounded the signal to charge. As he broke through the enemy's lines, his elephant stumbled and fell. Queen Suriyothai quickly maneuvered her elephant in front of the oncoming Burmese. She fought bravely and saved the king's life, but in the process she was killed. After the battle, the grieving king retrieved her body. Today, her ashes are said to be preserved in a shrine in Ayutthaya province. The people of Thailand regard Queen Suriyothai as one of their greatest national heroes.

system that gave different rights and privileges to individuals based upon their rank in society, from slave to prince.

Located in a rich rice-growing area with easy access by river to the ocean, Ayutthaya developed into a global commercial and trading center. Ayutthaya had long-standing trading partners such as India, Persia, and China. Later, it acquired new partners in the form of Portuguese, Dutch, English, Spanish, and French trading companies. The court of Ayutthaya exchanged ambassadors with the French court as well as with the imperial courts of India, Japan, and China.

Some western visitors to Ayutthaya declared the capital, with its magnificent palaces and temples, one of the most beautiful cities in the world. As time went on, more and more of these visitors began to refer to the kingdom by its regional nickname—Siam. That became the name that stuck in the West.

Westerners Arrive

In 1511, the first European ships, flying Portuguese flags, sailed up the Chao Phraya River to the Ayutthaya capital. In the seventeenth century, ships bearing Dutch, English, Spanish, and French traders began arriving. French missionaries also arrived. At first, Ayutthaya welcomed the newcomers, with their strange ways and frightening weapons. A few foreigners were even employed in the king's service. But little by little, the royal family grew to mistrust some of these foreigners who seemed very concerned with converting their Buddhist subjects to Christianity. In 1688, a new royal family came to power. This ruling family was less welcoming to foreigners. For the next century, Asians such as Chinese, Malays, Indonesians, and Indians carried on much of the trade with Ayutthaya.

In the meantime, Ayutthaya had to deal with a more pressing threat. For decades, territorial disputes with Burma had led to periodic wars. When Burmese troops attacked in 1767, they razed Ayutthaya, burning its treasured buildings, artworks, and religious artifacts. Ninety thousand Thais, including the king and his family, were captured and deported to Burma. En route, the king died. Once again, Thailand lost its independence.

Thonburi

In 1767, a Chinese army launched a surprise attack against Burma from the north. The Burmese were forced to move their troops to fight that battle. A brilliant Thai general named Taksin quickly raised an army and drove the thinned-out Burmese occupiers from Ayutthaya. With Ayutthaya in ruins, Taksin decided to relocate the capital. He chose Thonburi, a fortified village near the mouth of the Chao Phraya River, opposite present-day Bangkok. Then he had himself declared king.

A statue of Taksin graces a park in the city of Chanthaburi.

Over time, King Taksin recovered all the Thai territory that had previously been lost to the Burmese. Then he pushed the kingdom's borders into northeastern Cambodia and Laos. Being half Thai and half Chinese, Taksin encouraged enterprising Chinese merchants and craftspeople to settle in Thonburi. Thonburi flourished. Taksin also was a promoter of Buddhism and Thai literature and art. Over time, however, he became cruel and dictatorial. In 1782, members of his military assassinated him.

A view of Bangkok in 1846. Bangkok grew quickly throughout the 1800s.

The Chakri Dynasty

In Taksin's place, a general named Chao Phraya Chakri ascended the throne. He was the founder of the Chakri dynasty, to which all of Thailand's subsequent rulers have belonged, and is now known as Rama I.

As one of his first acts, Rama I relocated his capital from Thonburi to the small fishing village of Bangkok, just east across the Chao Phraya River. He reasoned that since most Burmese attacks had come from the west, forcing his enemies to cross a river to reach his capital would make the capital that much harder to assault. In Bangkok, he hoped to recapture the glory and splendor of Sukhothai and Ayutthaya. From the ruins of these former capitals, Rama I recovered images of Buddha, and other relics, and transported them to Bangkok. Structures designed in the Ayutthaya style arose all over the city. These included the majestic Grand Palace and the dazzling Temple of the Emerald Buddha. Rama I also supported the arts. One of the great literary creations of this period was the *Ramakien*, the Thai verse adaptation of the Indian epic *Ramayana*.

Dealing with the West

In the early nineteenth century, Rama I's successors faced new challenges. European nations were looking to Southeast Asia as the next place for colonial expansion. Under pressure from these nations, principally Great Britain, Rama II (ruled 1809–1824) warily reopened Siam's doors to Westerners. Meanwhile, he began the reconstruction of the Wat Arun (Temple of Dawn) on the Chao Phraya River.

Rama III (ruled 1824–1851) continued work on Wat Arun. He introduced Western medicine to Thailand and boosted foreign trade. The year he became king, British ships attacked Burma, and the British took control of some coastal provinces. Rama III did not want Siam to become involved in a dispute with the British about trade, so in 1826 he agreed to a treaty that gave special trading rights to British merchants in his kingdom. Seven years later, Siam signed a similar treaty with the United States.

Modernizing Siam

In 1851, Rama IV (known as Mongkut) became Siam's new ruler. He was a humane, compassionate, and intellectually curious man.

Rama III was known for being a devout Buddhist and was devoted to feeding the poor.

He studied Western languages, including English, and was extremely interested in science and technology. (In 1848, he designed and built a steam engine.) A pious Buddhist, he spent twenty-seven years as a monk.

Mongkut sought to open up his country to Western influences. He built new roads and canals, modernized his army, and reformed the education system. Rejecting age-old atti-

"Grandma Mo" Frees the Hostages

In 1827, troops from Laos invaded Siam, as Thailand was known then. They captured the city of Nakhon Ratchasima and began marching its inhabitants back toward their kingdom, some 240 miles (390 km) to the north. The Laotians wanted to force the king of Siam to free Laos from Siamese control in exchange for release of the hostages.

It is said that among the prisoners was a woman called Khun Ying Mo. A woman of great intelligence and a sharp reader of people, Khun Ying Mo was also fearless. Early on in the march, she emerged as the spokesperson for the captives. Using tricks and delaying tactics, she succeeded in slowing the march to a crawl. She also persuaded the Laotians to let the Siamese use cooking and farm tools that she then secretly had turned into weapons. Armed with these makeshift weapons, the Siamese surprised and defeated their captors. In recognition of Khun Ying Mo's role in ending the hostage crisis, the king awarded her the title *Thao Suranari*, meaning "The Brave Lady." Most Thais, however, refer to her as Ya Mo, or "Grandma Mo."

Khun Ying Mo is a revered symbol of national pride. Today, a statue of Thao Suranari stands in the center of Nakhon Ratchasima. Thais come from all over to pay their respects. Visitors remove their shoes, climb the steps leading up to the statue, and then place flowers, decorations, and burning sticks of incense around it. A festival in Thao Suranari's honor is held each year in the spring.

tudes toward the monarch as a god-king, Mongkut allowed his subjects to look upon his face directly.

Beginning in 1855, Mongkut concluded a series of treaties with Great Britain and other Western powers that opened the kingdom to wider international trade. Western traders were encouraged to make investments and open companies

King Mongkut and Queen Rampoei in the 1850s

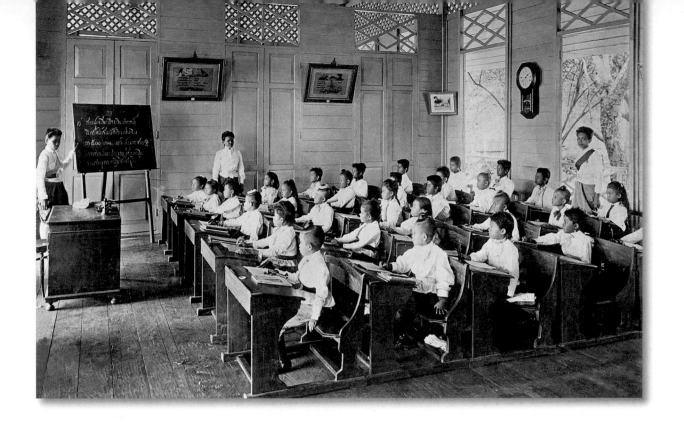

Thai children at school in 1907.

in Bangkok. Regular shipping services were established to Singapore, China, and other places. Exports of Thai products, such as rice, brought revenue to the government, which was, in turn, able to be invested in more services to help modernize the economy.

Upon Mongkut's death in 1868, leadership of Siam passed into the hands of his fifteen-year-old son Chulalongkorn, also known as Rama V. Chulalongkorn ruled the country until 1910. Considered one of Thailand's greatest rulers, Chulalongkorn abolished slavery and forced labor for the state. He built Siam's first hospital, instituted national postal and telegraph systems, and constructed roads and railroads. A firm believer in the power of education, Chulalongkorn created a national public school system and encouraged Thai students to study abroad.

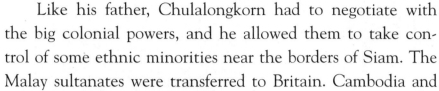

As a young man, Vajiravudh studied law and history at Oxford University in England.

Like his father, Chulalongkorn had to negotiate with the big colonial powers, and he allowed them to take control of some ethnic minorities near the borders of Siam. The Malay sultanates were transferred to Britain. Cambodia and Laos came under French rule. Today, Thailand honors the memory of Chulalongkorn with a national holiday on the anniversary of his death.

Chulalongkorn's son Vajiravudh (Rama VI), the first Siamese king to be educated abroad, was both a Westernizer and a strong nationalist. Until his reign, most Thais had only one name. In 1913, he ordered all Siamese to take a second, family name. In 1917, Vajiravudh established the nation's first university in Bangkok, Chulalongkorn University, named after his father. Four years later, he decreed that all Siamese children complete at least a primary school educa-

tion. In response to an influx of Chinese into the country, Vajiravudh required all students to become proficient in the Thai language. He also established organizations such as the Thai Boy Scouts.

End of the Absolute Monarchy

From the thirteenth century to the early twentieth century, Thai kings were absolute monarchs. Whatever they commanded became law. As the twentieth century wore on, though, an increasing number of Thais began to yearn for a say in their own governance: They wanted democracy. Matters came to a head in 1932. A group of officials and army officers rose up against King Prajadhipok (Rama VII) in a military coup. The king, who was absent from Bangkok at the time, quickly agreed to the rebels' terms. The absolute monarchy was abolished and replaced by a democratic constitutional monarchy. King Prajadhipok was allowed to rule again, but his powers became limited and were defined in Thailand's first constitution.

The new government got off to a shaky start. It was dominated by military figures who had led the coup. In 1933, a cousin of the king hatched a royalist plot to overturn the constitution. It was quashed by the military. King Prajadhipok had not been involved in the plot, but he decided to give up the throne anyway. He was succeeded by his ten-year-old nephew, Ananda Mahidol (Rama VIII). One of the military men who foiled the plot was Phibun Songkhram, who rose to become minister of defense in 1934 and premier in 1938, assuming near-dictatorial powers. In 1939, as one of his first acts, Phibun changed the name of the country from Siam to Thailand.

Phibun had long been an admirer of Imperial Japan. During World War II (1939–1945), he allowed Japanese troops to use Thai territory to invade Burma and the British-controlled part of the Malay Peninsula. In 1942, Phibun declared war on Japan's enemies, which included Great Britain, Canada, and the United States. But anti-Japanese feelings grew in Thailand. Toward the end of the war, Phibun stepped down because of his pro-Japanese actions.

In June 1946, one of the most puzzling events in modern Thai history occurred. King Ananda was found in his palace bedroom, dead from a gunshot wound. The circumstances of his death remain a mystery to this day. His younger brother Bhumibol Adulyadej ascended to the throne as Rama IX. He has been Thailand's ruler ever since, though he is in ailing health.

Modern Times

After World War II, both Thailand and the United States were concerned about the threat of communism in Asia. This led to the two nations becoming allies. Thailand gave the United States permission to build military bases on its soil, and during the Vietnam War in the 1960s and 1970s, Thai troops fought alongside American forces. Massive amounts of

Ananda Mahidol spent much of his childhood in Switzerland.

American military and economic aid poured into Thailand. This enabled the Thai government to invest in projects that spurred its industrial and agricultural growth. Between 1950 and 1980, farming prospered, driving up exports. Manufacturing and service industries also expanded, giving Thailand one of the highest economic growth rates in the world. Between 1991 and 1995, Thailand's exports nearly doubled in value.

Not all Thais benefited equally from this growth. The gap between rich and poor in Thailand widened. More than four million Thais left rural areas to crowd into cities in search of better jobs. Even so, the proportion of Thais living in poverty dropped from 23 percent in 1981 to less than 10 percent in 1994.

U.S. troops trained with Thai forces in Thailand in the early 1960s.

In 1997, Thailand's boom went bust. Companies cut back on production and laid off workers. Thailand adopted strict measures to halt the economic free fall, and by early 1999 the economy had begun improve.

Democracy on a Seesaw

Throughout much of King Bhumibol Adulyadej's reign, Thailand has struggled to make its democracy work. The 1932 revolution gave Thailand its first written constitution, but it did not ensure free and fair elections. For the next half century, the makeup of Thai governments was usually determined by the military, and the country went through more than a dozen versions of its constitution. When the military once again took over in 1971 and threw out the latest constitution, opposition among students and members of the educated middle class grew. In 1973, pro-democracy demonstrations were brutally suppressed by the military government. More than a hundred protesters were killed. Public outcry forced the military to call new elections, which took place in 1975. This first freely elected government in years was ousted by the military the following fall.

For the next twenty-five years, Thailand's democracy continued to seesaw between governments installed by generals and governments elected by the people. In the 2001 general election, a business tycoon named Thaksin Shinawatra, promising economic reforms, won a landslide victory. Thaksin's support came from the rural poor in the north and from the business community. He was unpopular among the urban middle class and Bangkok's elite. During his term as prime minister, the Thai

Protesters demonstrated against the government in 2008, claiming it was still under the control of former prime minister Thaksin Shinawatra.

economy regained the momentum it had lost in the financial crisis. In 2005, voters rewarded him by returning him to power.

Then things started to unravel for him. Accusations of corruption against Thaksin led to his ouster by the military in 2006, and in 2008 he fled the country to escape prosecution. Since then, pro- and anti-Thaksin demonstrators have frequently taken to the streets. Thaksin's supporters identify themselves by wearing red shirts, and his opponents wear yellow shirts.

Although the military restored civilian rule in 2008, tensions remained high. In 2010 a massive red-shirt demonstration in Bangkok ended in bloodshed, with dozens of protesters killed and hundreds more wounded. Yet despite the opposition of the military, a pro-Thaksin party headed by Yingluck Shinawatra, Thaksin's younger sister, won a majority in parliament in 2011.

Yingluck faced intense hostility from the anti-Thaksin movement, whose members believed that she was doing her brother's bidding rather than acting independently. In early May 2014, the Thai Constitutional Court ousted her because it said she had unlawfully reassigned a government official. Many outside observers believed the court's move was politically motivated. It was the third time since 2008 that the court had removed a prime minister who supported Thaksin. Then, two weeks later, the acting prime minister who had replaced her was also forced from office when the military seized control of the government.

Hostilities between supporters and opponents of Thaksin continue to simmer. Only time will tell whether Thailand will emerge from this period with a stronger democracy.

Yingluck Shinawatra was Thailand's first female prime minister.

CHAPTER 5

A Fragile Democracy

THAILAND HAS BEEN A CONSTITUTIONAL MONARCHY since 1932. Under a constitutional monarchy, a king or queen is the head of state but does not lead the government, and the monarch's powers are limited. Since 1782, all monarchs in Thailand have come from one ruling family: the Chakri dynasty. Until recently, only males could occupy the throne, but females are now allowed to rule.

The institution of the monarchy commands great respect in Thai society. Pictures of the king and the royal family hang in almost every home and office. The king's birthday and coronation and the queen's birthday are public holidays. Public actions that show disrespect toward the monarchy are not tolerated. A person who insults, spreads gossip about, or threatens a member of the royal family may be jailed for up to fifteen years. The government operates a special police unit that monitors the Internet for evidence of such offenses.

Opposite: **The Grand Palace has been the official residence of Thailand's leaders since 1782. King Bhumibol Adulyadej lives elsewhere, however, and uses the Grand Palace only for official events.**

The Longest Reign

King Bhumibol Adulyadej (Rama IX) is the world's longest-ruling monarch. Born in 1927, he has occupied the throne since 1946. Under the Thai constitution, King Bhumibol has little concrete power. Yet what he lacks in constitutional authority he makes up in force of personality.

King Bhumibol tends to avoid involvement in Thailand's volatile politics. On rare occasions, though, he has used his popularity to help defuse difficult political situations. He has also used his powers of persuasion to get some farm tribes in northern Thailand to shift from growing poppies to other crops. Poppies can be used to make illegal drugs such as heroin.

King Bhumibol has diverse interests. He speaks three languages in addition to Thai, plays jazz saxophone and clarinet, composes music, paints, sculpts, and writes poetry and scholarly articles. His official residence is the Grand Palace in Bangkok. However, he and Queen Sirikit usually stay at the Chitralada Palace

in Bangkok or the Klai Kangwon Palace (Palace Far from Worries) in the beach resort of Hua Hin. The royal family pays the cost of maintaining the royal palaces and their lifestyle themselves.

Constitutional Framework

The constitution of 1932 established Thailand as a parliamentary democracy. Today, however, rule by the people has yet to become an established way of life. The Thai military, which helped set the nation on the road to democracy, has repeatedly intervened in Thai politics—sometimes to suppress protests, and sometimes to overturn election results it didn't like. Such interference has given Thailand a kind of on-again, off-again democracy. The country has seen sixteen revisions of its constitution since 1932. Thailand's seventeenth constitution

Symbol of the King

The white elephant is a traditional symbol of the Thai kings. It has long been prized as a sign of wealth and happiness in the realm. The more white elephants a king had, the more promising his fortunes. Today in Thailand, anyone who discovers a white elephant in the wild must report the find to the ministry of interior. If the elephant meets the standards for a royal white elephant, it automatically becomes the property of the king. The royal family currently owns at least eleven white elephants, one of which can be seen at the Dusit Zoo in Bangkok.

was drafted by a military-led government in 2007, and later approved by a public vote. Prior to the vote, the military made it illegal for anyone to criticize its proposed draft in public.

Thai soldiers guard a building in Bangkok after the Thai military seized control of the government in May 2014.

The 2007 constitution keeps the basic governmental structure of previous constitutions. It divides the government into three branches: executive, legislative, and judicial.

Prem Tinsulanonda (far left, front) has been the president of the Privy Council since 1998. Prior to that he had served as Thailand's prime minister.

The Executive Branch

The executive branch consists of the king and his Privy Council, an eighteen-member body that advises the king, and the prime minister and the Council of Ministers.

The head of the Thai government is the prime minister. The prime minister proposes and administers laws and runs the government on a day-to-day basis. Under the constitution, he or she must be an elected member of the House of Representatives. In most cases, the leader of the party that wins the general election automatically becomes the prime minister. By law, the prime minister cannot serve longer than two consecutive four-year terms.

The prime minister is assisted by the thirty-five-member council of ministers. The council advises the prime minister

A woman casts a ballot in 2014. Thailand was the first country in eastern Asia to grant women the right to vote, in 1932.

and carries out the government's policies. Each minister has responsibility for a different governmental function, such as defense, finance, education, and public health.

The Legislative Branch

The legislative branch (or parliament) is known as the National Assembly. It is made up of two bodies: the Senate and the House of Representatives. To become law, a bill must pass both houses and be approved by the king. The king's approval, today, is simply a formality.

Members of the National Assembly meet in the Parliament House of Thailand in Bangkok.

The National Anthem

The music to the Thai national anthem, "Phleng Chat" ("National Song"), was composed by Phra Jenduriyang in 1932. Seven years later, lyrics by Luang Saranuprabhandi were added. By law, all people in Thailand in public places are required to stand for the national anthem. The anthem is played at eight o'clock every morning and six o'clock every evening in schools, offices, and on all broadcast media. It is also played in movie theaters and other public places prior to performances.

Transliteration of Thai lyrics

Pra thet thai ruam luead nu'a chat chu'a thai,
Pen pra cha rat pha thai kho'ng thai thuk suan,
Yu dam rong khong wai dai thang muan,
Duay thai luan mai rak sa mak khi,
Thai ni rak sa ngop tae thu'ng rop mai khlat,
Ek ka raj ja mai hai khrai khom khi,
Sa la luead thuk yat pen chat p'hli,
Tha loeng pra thet chat thai tha wi mi chai ch'yo!

English translation

Thailand embraces in its bosom all people of Thai blood.
Every inch of Thailand belongs to the Thais.
It has long maintained its sovereignty,
Because the Thais have always been united.
The Thai people are peace-loving,
But they are no cowards at war.
They shall allow no one to rob them of their independence,
Nor shall they suffer tyranny.
All Thais are ready to give up every drop of blood
For the nation's safety, freedom, and progress.

Justices on the Supreme Court listen to a case in 2010.

The House of Representatives has 500 members. This includes 375 people elected to represent their party of the country. The remaining 125 are based on proportional representation. This means that these seats are divided up by political party according to the percentage of the total vote that party received in the election. House members serve four-year terms.

The Senate has 150 seats. Of these, 76 are elected by popular vote and 74 are appointed by a panel of judges and government officials. Senate members are not permitted to be current members of political parties or to have served in government during the previous five years. Senators serve six-year terms.

The Judicial Branch

There are three levels to the Thai trial court system. Civil and criminal cases are tried in Courts of First Instance. These courts handle the largest number of cases. The Court of Appeals can review judgments made by these trial courts. The Supreme Court is the highest court in the land. It has the final say on the merits of decisions made by the Court of Appeals. In addition, Thailand has a separate Constitutional Court that rules on constitutional issues.

National Government of Thailand

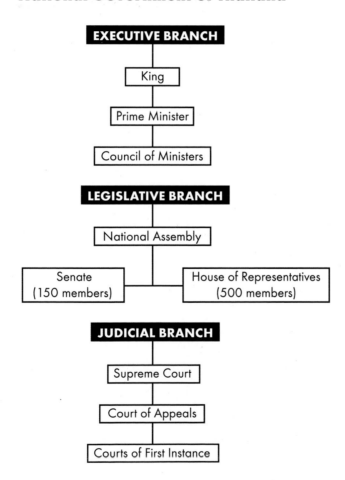

The National Flag

Prior to 1917, Thailand's flag featured a white elephant against a red background. In 1917, a new flag was introduced that remains the national flag of Thailand. It is composed of horizontal stripes of red, white, and blue. The flag's two red stripes, across the top and bottom, symbolize the land and its people. The adjacent white stripes symbolize the purity of Buddhism, the nation's dominant religion. The wide blue band across the center represents the monarchy. The national flag is raised every morning at eight o'clock and lowered every evening at six o'clock.

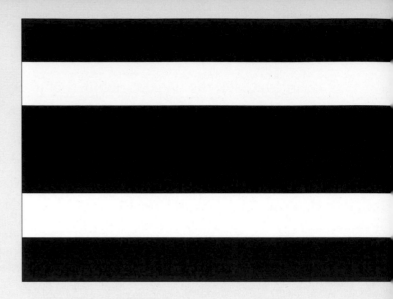

Local Government

Thailand has seventy-six provinces, including metropolitan Bangkok, which is its own province. Each province, except for Bangkok, is headed by a governor appointed by the minister of the interior. Bangkok's governor is elected by popular vote. Provinces are subdivided into 795 districts, 81 subdistricts, 7,255 rural subdistricts, and tens of thousands of villages. Each rural subdistrict is made up of between two and twenty-eight villages.

Large cities are governed by a mix of elected and appointed officials. Rural subdistricts are run by committees of local leaders who are responsible for matters such as maintaining roads and setting budgets. Village heads maintain village records, mediate minor disputes, and act as village advocates in dealings with higher levels of government. To serve as a village head, a person must have lived in a village for at least six months, be at least twenty-five years old, and be able to read. Women were first permitted to be village heads in 1983.

Bustling Bangkok

More than eight million people live in the hot, glittery, energetic, noisy city of Bangkok, Thailand's capital. Located near the mouth of the Chao Phraya and sprawling in all directions, it is the transportation hub of the region and the entire country. Bangkok is the economic, political, and cultural powerhouse of the country. All industrial, financial, and commercial life in Thailand revolves around the city.

Bangkok was chosen as the new capital of Siam in 1782. The origin of the name Bangkok has never been satisfactorily established. One common interpretation is that the name comes from the Thai words *bang* and *makok*, meaning "village of wild plums." Thais, however, refer to their city as Krung Thep, which is shorthand for what Thais proudly claim as the longest place-name in the world. The formal name for Bangkok, in Thai, is: *Krung Thep Mahanakhon*

Amon Rattanakosin Mahinthara Ayutthaya Mahadilok Phop Noppharat Ratchathani Burirom Udomratchaniwet Mahasathan Amon Piman Awatan Sathit Sakkathattiya Witsanukam Prasit. It translates to: "City of Angels, Great City of Immortals, Magnificent City of the Nine Gems, Seat of the King, City of Royal Palaces, Home of Gods Incarnate, Erected by Visvakarman at Indra's Behest."

Bangkok today is a bustling mix of old and new. Towering skyscrapers fill the business districts. Bangkok is one of the world's top tourist destinations. Visitors come from all over the world to see the Grand Palace and historic Buddhist temples such as Wat Arun and Wat Pho.

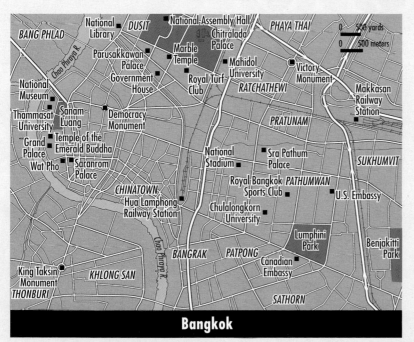

Bangkok

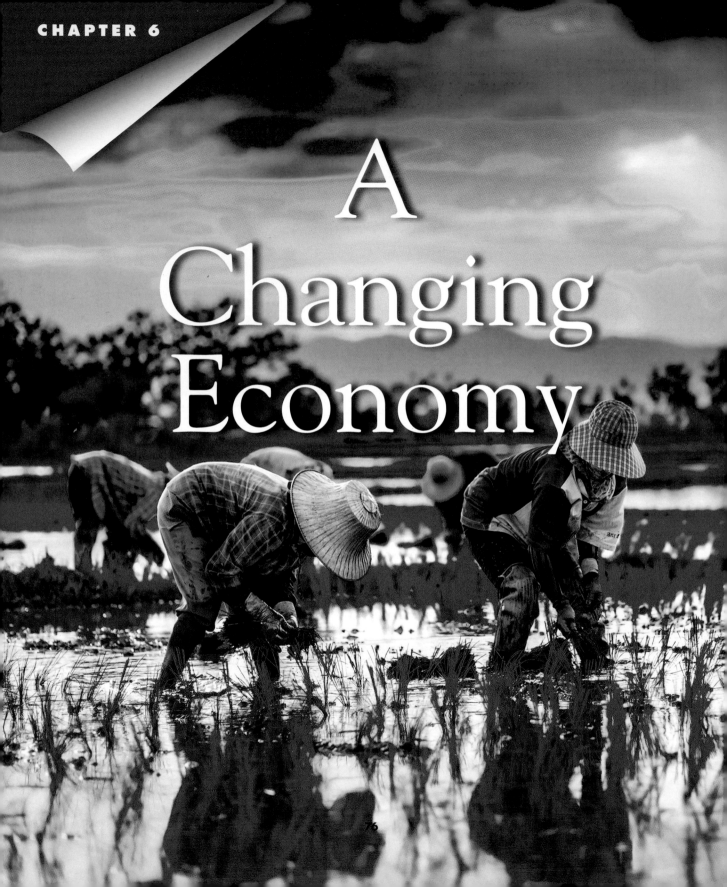

CHAPTER 6

A Changing Economy

THAILAND HAS THE SECOND-LARGEST ECONOMY IN Southeast Asia, after Indonesia. Historically, the Thai economy was based on farming and harvesting natural resources. Rice, rubber, tin, hardwoods, animal hides, and jewels were produced for sale abroad. Seaports and coastal cities flourished as trading centers for merchants from the Middle East, India, and China. In the twentieth century, the Thai government encouraged a shift from farming to manufacturing. Beginning in the 1960s, textiles, consumer goods, and, later, electronic components were being produced for shipment overseas. Today, manufacturing and services drive the economy.

Opposite: **Farmers planting rice in Thailand. About 38 percent of the labor force in Thailand works in agriculture.**

Agriculture

As late as 1980, agriculture employed about three-fourths of Thai workers and accounted for more than two-thirds of the country's export earnings. By 2012, the importance of agriculture in the economy had declined sharply. Agriculture contributed only about one-eighth of export earnings and provided only about 12

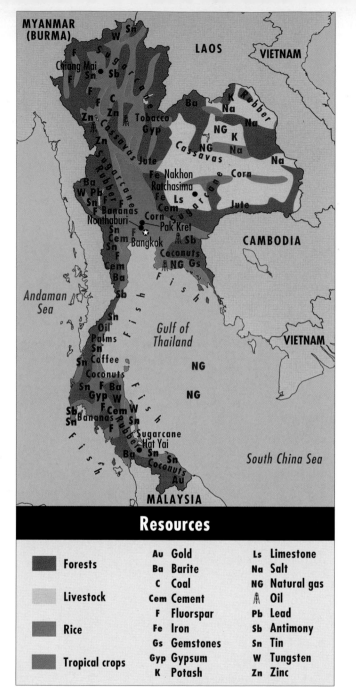

Resources

▮ Forests	Au	Gold	Ls	Limestone
	Ba	Barite	Na	Salt
	C	Coal	NG	Natural gas
▮ Livestock	Cem	Cement	⚒	Oil
	F	Fluorspar	Pb	Lead
▮ Rice	Fe	Iron	Sb	Antimony
	Gs	Gemstones	Sn	Tin
	Gyp	Gypsum	W	Tungsten
▮ Tropical crops	K	Potash	Zn	Zinc

percent of Thailand's gross domestic product (GDP), the total value of the goods and services a nation produces.

Rice is Thailand's most important crop. It is a staple of the Thai diet and Thailand's top agricultural export. For decades Thailand has been one of the world's largest rice exporters, shipping more than 6.5 million tons (5.9 million metric tons) annually. Its main rice-producing areas are the Chao Phraya River basin and the Khorat Plateau. Other valuable export crops include rubber, sugarcane, coconut, cassava, corn, mangoes, pineapples, cashews, soybeans, and flowers. Exports of shrimp, fish, and fish products are also growing.

Manufacturing and Mining

The industrial sector of the Thai economy benefited from the government's pro-manufacturing policies in the decades following World War II. In 2012, industrial production grew at an annual rate of 7.2 percent and accounted for 43.6 percent of GDP. Thai industries employ nearly 14 percent of the workforce. Most export-oriented firms operate in or around Bangkok, but an increasing number of cities in the northeast and north, including Nakhon Ratchasima and Chiang Mai, have emerged as regional manufacturing centers. Thailand exports electronics, motor vehicles, computer components, electric appliances, processed foods, telecommunications equipment, furniture, plastics, footwear, textiles, and garments.

Construction and mining together provided 4.3 percent of the country's GDP in 2012. Thailand is the world's second-largest exporter of both gypsum and tungsten. Other mines and quarries yield coal, zinc, tin, fluorite, limestone, and marble. Rubies and sapphires are mined on the east coast of the Malay Peninsula, and natural gas deposits have been found offshore.

What Thailand Grows, Makes, and Mines

AGRICULTURE (2010)

Sugarcane	68,807,800 metric tons
Rice	31,597,200 metric tons
Cassava	22,005,700 metric tons

MANUFACTURING

Motor vehicles (2013)	2,532,577 vehicles
Textiles (2010)	833,000 metric tons
Electronics (2011)	US$55,000,000,000 in export revenues

MINING

Lignite (2011)	20,500,000 metric tons
Gypsum (2009)	8,500,000 metric tons
Zinc (2009)	34,000 metric tons

Services

The service sector has contributed the largest share of Thailand's GDP since 1993. Currently, the sector brings in more than 44 percent of the annual national income. A wide range of occupations and professions are represented in this sector: teachers, bankers, doctors, artists, carpenters, cooks, bus drivers, and government workers, among others.

The service sector includes many kinds of workers, including doctors and nurses.

Measuring Up

Thailand began using the metric system to survey land for tax purposes as early as 1896. In 1923, it officially adopted the system as its standard for measurements. Ancient Thai methods for making measurements were not entirely abandoned, however. Even today, the old system of measuring land and property, which uses traditional units such as the *rai*, *ngan*, and *wah*, is still used, especially in rural areas. Under this system, 1 rai = 4 ngan = 400 square wah = 17,222 square feet (1,600 square meters) = 0.40 acres (0.16 hectares).

In addition, the weight of gold is almost always measured in a unit called baht. (This baht is unrelated to the currency baht.) One baht of gold is equal to 0.54 ounces (15.3 grams).

The attractions of Bangkok and ancient cities such as Chiang Mai and Ayutthaya and the lure of scenic ocean getaways in the south have made tourism a key driver of Thailand's service sector. In 2007, money from tourism accounted for 7 percent of the GDP. In no other Asian country does tourism play such a large role in the economy.

Transportation and Telecommunications

Travel and communications in Thailand have improved greatly in recent decades. The railway system now has more than 2,530 miles (4,072 km) of lines. The nation is crisscrossed by 112,000 miles (180,000 km) of roads and highways. For the first time, some of these roads reach into the once isolated hill country of the north.

Floating Markets

Tourists travel to Thailand to relax on the beaches and explore ancient temples, but many also come to buy fruit. One of the most colorful places to do this is at the Damnoen Saduak Floating Market, north of Bangkok. The land near Bangkok is threaded with rivers and canals. These waterways were traditionally the best transportation routes, so Thai farmers would carry their crops to market in boats. There, they would sell their fruits and vegetables to people who gathered along the shore. Over the years, many floating markets shut down as more and more Thais began buying produce at supermarkets, but some remain active. Merchants still sell their produce from boats at float-

ing markets such as the one at Damnoen Saduak, but most shoppers today are tourists rather than Thais. The floating markets remain, however, a fascinating glimpse into the way many Thais once lived.

Thais are also increasingly connected to one another and to the world by modern telecommunications. Virtually everyone in Thailand owns a cell phone, and about one in four Thais has Internet access. Traffic on the Thai Internet is monitored by the government for unlawful speech and criminal activity.

Thailand has more than five hundred radio stations and 110 television stations. The six TV stations that serve Bangkok are controlled by the government, including two that are owned and operated by the military. All these TV stations are required by law to broadcast government-produced news programs twice daily. In recent years, a number of community-based low-power radio stations have sprung up to provide alternatives to government-controlled programming. However, sometimes these stations have run afoul of the government and been shut down. The subject matter on Thai TV ranges from game shows, comedies, and dramas to talk shows, sports, and educational programs.

Unlike Thai television, the newspapers in Thailand are relatively free of government control. Readers have a choice of dozens of newspapers printed in Thai, English, or other languages. Almost all daily papers are published in Bangkok and distributed across the country.

Money Facts

The baht is the basic unit of money in Thailand. Coins come in values of 1, 5, and 10 baht. Bills have values of 10, 20, 50, 100, 500, and 1,000 baht. One baht is made up of 100 *satang*. The satang only comes in coins. The 1-, 5-, and 10-satang coins are rarely seen in circulation, but the 25- and 50-satang coins are common.

On the front of every coin and bill is an image of King Bhumibol. His image is often adorned with other traditional symbols, such as the royal seal, the lotus flower sacred to Buddhism, or Garuda, the mythical half-man, half-bird creature. On the back of coins is a representation of the Grand Palace. The reverse side of banknotes commemorates historical figures and special events. The 50-baht note, for example, shows King Chulalongkorn, and the 500-baht bill bears a stamp celebrating the fiftieth anniversary of King Bhumibol's reign, which occurred in 1996. In 2014, 1 baht was worth US$0.031, and US$1.00 was worth 32 baht.

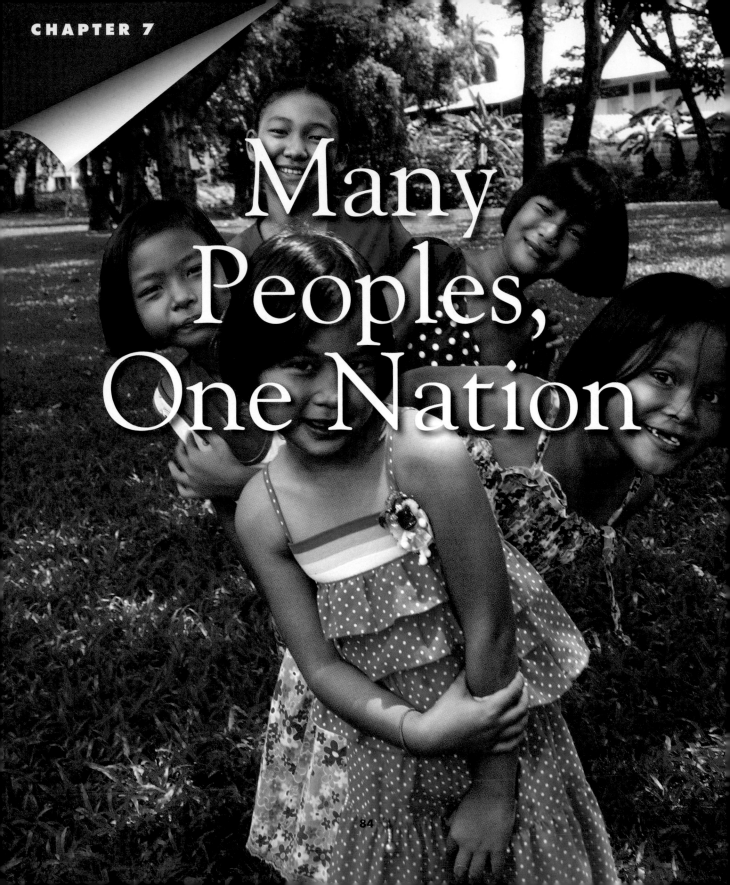

CHAPTER 7

Many Peoples, One Nation

THAILAND HAS ABOUT SEVENTY MILLION INHABITANTS, making it the twenty-first most populous country in the world. Ethnic Thais make up the vast majority of the population, about 75 percent. They are the descendants of the Tai-speaking tribes that rose to power in the region beginning in the late thirteenth century. Among the country's minorities are ethnic Chinese, Malays, Mon-Khmer, hill tribes, Indians, and Westerners.

Different Heritages

Although many minorities in Thailand retain aspects of their cultural identity, the ethnic boundaries between these groups and the Thai majority are not always clear-cut. A significant proportion of Thais have mixed ancestry. It is estimated, for example, that about 40 percent of the Thai population has at least one Chinese forebear.

Thailand's Ethnic Groups	
Thai	75%
Chinese	14%
Malay	3%
Other, including Mon-Khmer, hill tribes, Indians, and Westerners	8%

This blending of ethnicities has pushed Thai society toward greater uniformity. More than 85 percent of the people in Thailand speak a Thai language. Close to 95 percent have the same religion, Theravada Buddhism. In the twenty-first century, being Thai is becoming less a matter of ancestry than of cultural and national identification.

The Chinese

Chinese have been playing an important role in the economic and political life of Thailand since the sixteenth century. General Taksin, who became king of Thonburi in 1767, was himself the son of a Chinese immigrant. He actively encour-

The vast majority of people in Thailand are Theravada Buddhists. Many Thai boys become monks for a period of time.

Thais light incense and candles during a Chinese New Year celebration.

aged Chinese immigration and trade. The founder of the present ruling Chakri dynasty, King Rama I, was also part Chinese. Likewise, Thailand's previous three prime ministers have been of Chinese descent.

Today, about 14 percent of Thais are ethnically Chinese. They are well integrated into all levels of society. Nearly all speak Thai as their primary language, and almost all use a Thai rather than a traditional Chinese surname. Entrepreneurs of Chinese ancestry are influential in virtually all sectors of the Thai economy, including real estate, agriculture, banking and finance, and the retail and wholesale trades.

Malays

Unlike the Chinese, the Malay- and Yawi-speaking peoples who live in Thailand's southernmost provinces are not immigrants. They make up Thailand's largest native minority.

Before the region came under direct Siamese control in the early twentieth century, it was a semi-independent Muslim state. Because they speak different languages and have separate religious and political traditions, the Malays have been less integrated into Thai society and culture.

Malays in the Thai portion of the peninsula tend to work in fishing, tin mining, or tourism, or on oil palm or coconut plantations. Islamist political movements seeking greater regional self-rule for Malays, or even complete independence from Thailand, have been active in the lower provinces for some time.

Hill Tribes

In Thailand's northern and western provinces live a scattering of different groups, each with distinct customs, languages, spiritual beliefs, and styles of dress. Known collectively as the hill tribes, these groups have a total estimated population of more than one million. The largest of these tribes include the Karen, Hmong, Akha, Lahu, Lisu, and Mien. Most of these hill tribes are believed to have migrated to Thailand long ago from Myanmar, Tibet, Laos, and southern and western China.

The Karens, who live in northern and central Thailand, are the largest of the hill tribes, with a population of about four hundred thousand. Karens build bamboo houses that are raised on stilts to create a shelter below for their pigs, chickens, and buffalo. Most Karens grow rice and other crops. For clothing, unmarried Karen girls traditionally wear loose, white V-necked blouses, while married women can be identified by their boldly colored blouses and skirts. Men typically wear red or blue shirts with colorful contrasting colors. Karen tribeswomen are known for their skillful weaving, while men make instruments, animal bells, and tobacco pipes. Karen men are also considered expert elephant trainers. About one-fourth of Karens are Christian. The majority, however, are Buddhists who also practice animism. Animists believe in a world that is inhabited by good and evil spirits.

The Hmong live in houses that sit atop a kind of above-ground basement in which food is stored. Hmong women are known for their exquisite needlework and silver jewelry. Many Hmong sell these crafts to add to their farming income.

The Hmong people live in mountainous regions of China, Vietnam, Laos, and Thailand.

Tens of thousands of Akha people live in small villages high up in the northern mountains. Entrances to Akha villages are through elaborately carved wooden spirit gates, which the Akha believe have the power to ward off evil. Akha dwellings are built of logs and bamboo. They are typically raised on stilts and have steeply pitched thatched roofs. Traditional dress for women consists of wide leggings, a short

The gates to Akha villages are meant to ward off evil spirits and welcome good spirits.

black skirt with a beaded pouch, and a black jacket edged with embroidery. Tribeswomen also wear spectacular headdresses decorated with silver coins, beads, and feathers. Men wear baggy black pants and an embroidered loose black jacket.

Padaung people are recent migrants from Myanmar into northern Thailand. They make their living growing tanatep, a large leaf used to wrap Burmese cigars. Padaung people speak a Mon-Khmer language. Both men and women decorate their teeth with gold and wear distinctive woven bamboo belts around their waists. The Padaung people are best known to the outside world for the brass coils the women wear around their necks. A Padaung girl begins wearing these coils around age five. Over time, more and more coils are added until the weight of the metal forces down her collarbone. By the time a girl reaches adulthood, the accumulation of coils gives her the appearance of a stretched neck.

Brass coils appear to extend the necks of Padaung women to about 15 inches (38 cm).

Population of Largest Cities (2010 est.)

Bangkok	8,280,925
Nonthaburi City	262,158
Pak Kret	178,114
Hat Yai	158,007
Nakhon Ratchasima	142,645
Chiang Mai	142,632

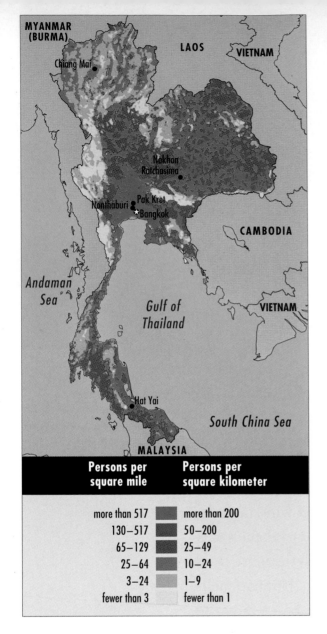

Persons per square mile	Persons per square kilometer
more than 517	more than 200
130–517	50–200
65–129	25–49
25–64	10–24
3–24	1–9
fewer than 3	fewer than 1

City and Country

Two out of three Thais today live in rural areas. As industrialization continues, however, the jobs of the future are likely to be found in the nation's cities. In the past half century, Bangkok grew the most quickly as rural Thais moved to cities. Now, other Thai cities are also beginning to feel the pressures on housing, jobs, education, and health care caused by rapid urbanization. Most of the people relocating from country to city are young adults.

Education

In Thailand today, every child is entitled to twelve years of free basic education. The first nine years are required for all children ages seven to sixteen; the final three are optional.

Basic schooling in Thailand consists of six years of primary education and six years of secondary education. Secondary school graduates who qualify on national tests are eligible to attend higher academic or vocational training institutions. Thailand currently has some 165 public and private colleges and universities, and more than 800 public and private vocational and technical schools and colleges. Roughly half of all university graduates in Thailand are women.

Until 1913, Thais used only one name—their given name—to identify themselves. Then King Vajiravudh ordered his subjects to take a family name.

Today, all Thais have two legal names. The word order is the same as it is in the West: The given name comes first and the family name second. Most given names are two or three syllables long. Family names are sometimes even longer. To simplify matters, parents usually give their babies single-syllable nicknames. These names often remain with them for life.

In informal conversation, Thais refer to one another by their first names. A term of respect, such as *Khun*—which stands for Mr., Mrs., or Miss—precedes the given name. In Thai, it is also customary to substitute a person's title for the pronouns *you, he,* or *she.* For example, you would say, "Is teacher going out?" instead of "Is *she* going out?"

Language

The Thai language is closely related to Lao and is one of about sixty languages in the larger Tai-Kadai language family. Many different dialects, or versions, of Thai exist, so the government chose one to serve as the standard language of education and communication. Known as Standard (or Siamese) Thai, it is based on the dialect spoken by twenty million people in the Chao Phraya Valley. Nearly every person in Thailand knows how to speak and write Standard Thai.

Like Chinese, Thai is a tonal language. In tonal languages, the meaning of a word can change depending on the way the voice sounds when it is spoken. Thai has five tones: high, low, middle, rising, and falling. For example, the word *kau* has five different meanings—news, white, rice, mountain, or he/she/it—depending on its tone. Thai is also complicated by the fact that there are five different levels to the language, each with its own specialized vocabulary: informal, used between relatives and friends; literary, used in formal writing; rhetorical, used in public speaking; religious, used when discussing Buddhism; and royal, used in all matters relating to the royal family.

The Thai alphabet is a flowery-looking script, said to have been created by King Ramkhamhaeng of Sukhothai in the late thirteen century. The language, which is written from left

Children relax with books at a public library in Bangkok.

to right, is very complicated. It has forty-four consonants and thirty-two vowels. Vowels appear above, below, before, or after the consonants they modify.

There are no spaces between words in the Thai language. Spaces are inserted only between clauses or sentences.

Say It in Thai

Note: In English spellings of Thai words, *ph* sounds like the *p* in police; *th* like the *t* in toast, and *kh* like the *k* in Korea.

Sawatdii khrap (said by a male)	Hello; good morning; good-bye
Sawatdii kha (said by a female)	Hello; good morning; good-bye
Sabaai dii reu?	How are you?
Sabaai dii.	I'm fine.
Khor thoot.	Excuse me.
Khorp khun.	Thank you.
Khun chu arai?	What is your name?
Khao chai mai?	Do you understand?
Phoot Thai mai dai.	I can't speak Thai.
Mai khao chai.	I don't understand.

Many Peoples, One Nation **95**

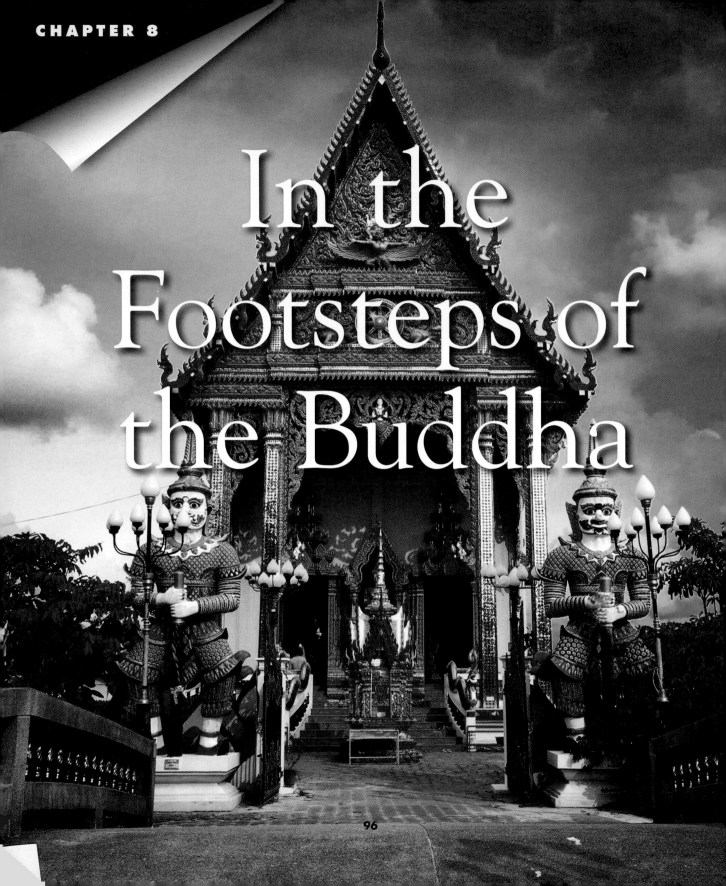

CHAPTER 8

In the Footsteps of the Buddha

THE VAST MAJORITY OF THAIS ARE BUDDHISTS. IT is hard to go anywhere in the country without seeing Buddhist monks in orange robes collecting food and alms donations daily. Over the centuries, Buddhism has shaped the moral, ethical, and cultural character of Thai society. The Buddhist *wat*, or temple complex, has traditionally been the focus of social and spiritual life in the countryside. Buddhism has also inspired much of the finest Thai art, architecture, literature, and music.

The Thai constitution does not specify a state religion. It does require, however, that the king be a Buddhist. It also guarantees religious freedom and bans religious discrimination.

Buddhism

Buddhism is less a religion than it is a way of life. Unlike Christianity, Islam, and Judaism, Buddhism is unconcerned about the meaning of life or the role of a god in the world's creation or oversight. Buddhists do not believe in Western conceptions of heaven or hell. Nor do they have a fixed day

Opposite: **There are more than forty thousand Buddhist temples in Thailand.**

Religion in Thailand	
Buddhism	93%
Islam	5%
Christianity	0.7%
Other	1.3%
(Confucianism, Hinduism, Judaism, Sikhism, Daoism, animism)	

The Buddha

Buddhism is based on the life and teachings of a man named Siddhartha Gautama. He is believed to have lived sometime during the sixth and fifth centuries BCE in what is now the India-Nepal border region. Born into a royal family, Siddhartha could have led a life of wealth and comfort. As a young man, however, he was so disturbed by human suffering that he vowed he would find its cause and a way to relieve it.

Abandoning his riches and family, he became a wanderer in search of truth. After years of meditation and self-discipline, he had a revelation that he believed gave him the answer. The way to end human misery, he said, was to conquer the emotions and desires to which all humans were enslaved. If people no longer craved money or fame or passion or power, and no longer feared death, these things could no longer hurt them. Such people would achieve a state of perfect inner peace called nirvana. Those who gathered to hear this holy man preach began calling him the Buddha, or "enlightened one."

for worship. Key to their beliefs is the idea, borrowed from Hinduism, that every living thing—from a snail to a person—undergoes an endless cycle of births, deaths, and rebirths known as reincarnation. The good or bad that you do in your present lifetime determines the quality of your life in the next. The Buddha taught that it was possible to end the cycle of birth and rebirth and all the suffering that came with it. The way to do so, he said, was to practice eight kinds of conduct and thinking: right understanding, right thought, right speech, right action, right livelihood, right effort, right mindfulness, and right contemplation. Mastering the techniques of this "Eightfold Path" would eventually bring the kind of enlightenment that the Buddha himself had experienced.

Making Merit

Buddhism teaches tolerance, compassion, and good behavior in this life to improve one's chances of being reborn with a nobler soul in the next. In Thailand, the practice of doing good deeds is called making merit. Making merit is a deeply ingrained part of Thai social behavior. Often, it takes the form of a public act that makes a material contribution to com-

In Thailand, Buddhist monks usually wear orange robes.

Thailand's Holiest Shrine

Perhaps the holiest Buddhist shrine in Thailand is Wat Phra Kaeo, popularly known as the Temple of the Emerald Buddha. Located on the grounds of the Royal Palace in Bangkok, Wat Phra Kaeo houses a six-hundred-year-old statue that is the most sacred artwork in Thailand. The Emerald Buddha is made of jade ("emerald" describes its color), stands 26 inches (66 cm) high, and sits atop a huge golden altar in the center of the temple.

No one is allowed to touch the statue except the Thai king, who comes to the temple three times a year to change the Buddha's ceremonial clothes. During the hot season, the statue wears a crown and a golden tunic decorated with diamonds. When the monsoon rains come, the Buddha is outfitted with a headdress and a golden robe flecked with blue. In the cooler season, the figure is covered with a golden shawl decorated with enamel.

munity life. Feeding monks, donating money to a wat, aiding the poor, and participating in Buddhist rituals are typical examples of how Thais make merit.

One way in which Thai men make merit and bring honor to their families is by becoming Buddhist monks. At peak times, an estimated 290,000 monks reside in Thailand's 32,000 wats. Only about 70,000 of these monks are full-time clergy, however. The remainder consists of young men who enter a monastery for a fixed period of time. The duration of their stay typically involves some multiple of three (for good luck): three days, three weeks, or three months. Traditionally, these young men go on retreat to the wat during the rainy season following their graduation from high school or in the months before they plan to marry.

A couple gives food to Buddhist monks.

While on retreat, these part-time monks dress and live like Buddhist clergy. They shave their heads, don orange robes, and go barefoot or wear sandals. At most, they eat two meals per day; there is no dinner in a wat. Food consists of rice or whatever other morsels they have collected from public donations that morning.

Monks lead a simple existence. Apart from their Buddhist garments, they are allowed to have no possessions other than an alms bowl, a razor, and a few necessities. They may not touch money, sing, or dance. Most of their time is spent meditating, studying Buddhist scriptures, and working around the temple grounds. By law, all employers must give a man time off to enter the monkhood, and big companies will usually pay his salary while he is on retreat.

Although women are not permitted to become monks in Thailand, they can shave their heads and eyebrows, don white robes, take vows, and become Buddhist nuns. Nuns do not have any legal standing in Thailand. Nor do they enjoy the same social status as monks. Unlike men, women cannot go on religious retreats without fear of losing their jobs. Monks ride free on public transportation, and nuns do not. Ordinary Thais sometimes donate less to nuns than to monks, because they believe that helping monks brings them more merit. On the grounds of a wat, nuns are routinely assigned to second-class living quarters. Prohibited from praying or eating with the monks, they spend their time meditating, studying, and chanting by themselves. In recent years, a group of activist nuns has been working to obtain full legal religious equality between men and women in Thailand—so far, without much success.

Religious Holidays

Thailand observes the following religious events as national holidays:

Makha Bucha, which usually occurs in February, is a day for spiritual purification and making merit. It commemorates a gathering of the Buddha's followers and one of his important teachings, known in Thailand as "The Heart of Buddhism." The highlight of the holiday is a candlelight procession by monks and other people.

Visakha Bucha, which usually falls in May, honors the birth, enlightenment, and death of the Buddha. Daytime ceremonies take place in temples; in the evening there is a candlelight procession.

Asanha Bucha, which usually takes place in July, celebrates the Buddha's first sermon following his enlightenment. People observe this day by donating offerings to temples and listening to sermons.

Khao Phansa Day, which usually falls in July, marks the beginning of a time for serious contemplation and meditation.

Role of the Wat

In Thai, the word *wat* means "monastery" as well as "temple." This is because the typical wat consists of a walled compound of buildings that provide both residences for monks and a place of worship for believers. Buildings in the compound usually feature distinctive architecture, such as sharply pointed roofs and elaborate decoration. In addition to its religious functions, a wat—especially one in a rural area—may also serve as a community center, a health clinic, a school, a library, a home for the elderly, and an information hotline center.

Monks living in wats have special cells where they can go to study or meditate. Some buildings also have large halls that are open to the public for Buddhist sermons. Tall golden spires atop some structures in the compounds house the ashes of famous monks or respected community figures.

Many different ceremonies take place at wats, including the ordination of monks, the hearing of confessions, and the annual

A young monk stands near his residence at a wat in Bangkok.

Young Muslim boys in Thailand enjoy ice cream cones.

distribution of new robes to monks. Funerals also take place on the grounds of the wat. Within a week after a person dies, monks, family members, and villagers gather to bless the body with holy water. Then the deceased's coffin is set afire, sending the body's ashes skyward. Although there are no regular religious services for congregations in Buddhism, members of the community are free to worship individually at a wat whenever they like.

Islam

About 5 percent of the Thai population is Muslim, or followers of Islam. Muslim communities can be found throughout the country, but the largest concentrations of Muslims are in Bangkok and in the southern Malay Peninsula. In four of Thailand's five southernmost provinces, Islam is the dominant religion. The majority of Muslims in these provinces are ethnic Malays.

As part of their religious duties, all Muslims are expected to make a pilgrimage to the holy shrines in Mecca, in Saudi Arabia, at least once in their lifetime. Some companies in Thailand grant their Muslim employees a paid leave to make this journey, which is known as the *hajj*.

Hinduism and Animism

Hindus make up only a tiny fraction of the Thai population, yet the influence of Hinduism on Thai Buddhism over the centuries has been profound. Siddhartha Gautama, the Buddha, was born a Hindu, and the Theravada tradition that was adopted in Thailand borrowed many beliefs and practices from Hinduism. Shrines to Hindu gods such as Brahma, Vishnu, Shiva, and Ganesha are found throughout the country. Garuda, a creature from Hindu mythology, is a national symbol. Hindu priests often oversee royal and state ceremonies. Thai births, marriages, and funerals blend Hindu and Buddhist rituals.

Spirit worship and animism are also widely practiced in Thailand, including by Buddhists and followers of other religions. In these beliefs, all of nature is inhabited by good spirits and bad spirits called *phi*. They can bring a person good luck or bad luck. Some phi are considered reincarnations of people who have died. *Chao*, or guardian spirits, help people sort out their spirit troubles. Many Thais build small "spirit houses" for these chao on posts outside their homes, which they stock with offerings of food, fresh flowers, and incense. For good measure, nearly all Thais carry at least one amulet or good-luck charm around with them wherever they go.

CHAPTER 9

Cultural Treasures

THAILAND HAS A LONG, RICH CULTURAL HERITAGE. Early on, its art, architecture, music, dance, literature, and crafts were shaped by the cultural traditions of India, China, Burma, and Cambodia. Thai ideas about beauty and the purpose of art were profoundly influenced by Hinduism and Buddhism as well. Artists in Thailand today often seek to blend classical Thai forms and themes with techniques and ideas borrowed from the West and elsewhere.

Opposite: **Traditional dancing uses many stylized hand movements.**

Sculpture and Architecture

Traditional Thai art is religious in origin. Prior to the twentieth century, almost all Thai sculpture consisted of statues of the Buddha. Working in highly polished stone, wood, or metal, sculptors made smooth representations of the Buddha that were intended to awe and inspire onlookers.

Everything about these statues, including the Buddha's posture, facial features, and hand gestures, had symbolic importance.

Beautiful paintings adorn the inside of many temples, including the Temple of the Emerald Buddha in Bangkok.

For example, all images of the Buddha reclining symbolize the Buddha's transition from life to nirvana. Ancient religious texts also gave Thai artists specific descriptions of the Buddha. He was said to have had an oval face, spiral curls, long hands and arms, and flat feet. Thai artists tried to follow these guidelines faithfully. They also produced exquisite artworks that illustrated the life of the Buddha and stories from Hindu mythology.

Present-day Thai sculptors work in diverse artistic traditions. One internationally renowned Thai painter and sculptor was Misiem Yipintsoi, who died in 1988. Her works, which often depict children, are on display in a sculpture garden near Bangkok.

The highest expression of classical Thai architecture is the Buddhist wat, or temple compound. Wats are often elaborately decorated. Beautiful murals cover their inner walls. Other surfaces are adorned with gold leaf, lacquer, and bits of inlaid mirrors, colored glass, pottery, and pearly shells. Every aspect of the wat was designed with religious symbolism in mind.

Painting

Classical Thai painting consisted mostly of temple and palace murals and book illustrations. Figures in these artworks were two-dimensional. Their size relative to one another was determined by their overall importance in the painting. The scenes in classical Thai painting are usually drawn from the life of the Buddha and Hindu literature.

Most Thai artists today have been schooled in modern as well as traditional styles. One of the best-known contemporary artists is Chakrapan Posayakrit, who paints portraits and scenes drawn from literature.

The Father of Modern Art in Thailand

The modern art movement in Thailand traces to the 1920s, when King Rama VI invited a noted Italian sculptor named Corrado Feroci (left) to Thailand to create bronze statues of national heroes. Feroci fell in love with Thailand and made it his home. Later, he had his name officially changed to a Thai one, Silpa Bhirasri. In 1933, he founded the Fine Arts School, which eventually came to be known as Silpakorn (Fine Arts) University. The purpose of the school was to instruct a new generation of Thai sculptors and painters in modern art. Silpa Bhirasri served as dean of the painting and sculpture faculty until his death in 1962 and is regarded as the father of modern art in Thailand.

Crafts

Thailand is renowned for its tradition of fine crafts. Pottery making is an ancient art in Thailand. In northeastern Thailand, archaeologists have dug up clay pots that date back to 3600 BCE. In the thirteenth century CE, Thai artisans in the kingdom of Sukhothai learned Chinese methods for making celadon porcelain. From this period on, Thailand's lustrous blue-green porcelain became a valuable export. In addition, almost every region of the country produces its own traditional style of pottery.

This celadon dish comes from Si Satchanalai in northern Thailand. It was made in the fourteenth or fifteenth century.

The art of making lacquered goods came to Thailand via Burma and China. Lacquer is a resin obtained from a tree. Lacquering involves applying more than a dozen thin coats of resin to a wooden surface, usually a box, bowl, plate, or piece of furniture. After each coat dries, the item is polished smooth. Eventually, the finish turns hard and glossy. Then the artist applies gold leaf or other decoration to the lacquered surface.

Thailand's north and northeast are centers for the production of high-quality silk. Hardy mulberry trees thrive in these regions. Silk is made from the cocoons of silkworms that dine solely on mulberry leaves. Following centuries-old practices, village women—mostly from hill tribes—tend to the mulberry trees, harvest the silkworm cocoons, and then spin and dye the thread. Thai silk is famous throughout the world for its durability, shimmering beauty, and exquisite designs.

A Thai artisan weaves silk. Thailand's silk industry is centered in the northern part of the country.

Another craft from northern Thailand is silver work. Skilled artisans in this region have been making silver boxes, bowls, tea sets, and jewelry for at least a thousand years. Silver goods are usually made from wire or thin sheets fashioned into lacy designs. Some feature raised patterns.

Performing Arts

Music figures prominently in Thai royal ceremonies, festivals, and dance and theatrical events. Thai classical music was originally played at court. Both this music and early Thai instruments were adapted from Khmer (Cambodian), Mon, and Indian models. Thais made their own versions of stringed instruments, drums, xylophones, cymbals, gongs, flutes, mouth organs, and oboes.

Classical Thai theater is very different from Western theater. In Thai theater, characters do not speak. Instead, stories are told through gestures and dance. Each step, glance, or gesture that a dancer makes carries a specific meaning known to the audience. A traditional Thai orchestra provides the background music.

Originally, all dance-dramas were performed only at court. Eventually, popular forms of these storytelling dances evolved for the entertainment of ordinary people. In classical productions, performers wear elaborate headdresses, silk costumes, and masks. Women tend to play female roles while men often portray clowns, monkeys, and ogres. Characters wearing masks usually represent good or evil spirits. The themes of traditional dance-dramas are generally taken from religious or folk classics.

Film

The first-known film showings in Thailand occurred in Bangkok in 1897. Three years later, a younger brother of King Chulalongkorn made Thailand's first motion picture. Today, the Thai film industry produces an average of about fifty feature films per year.

In 2000, *Fah talai jone* (*Tears of the Black Tiger*)—a parody of a Western—became the first Thai film to be shown at the prestigious Cannes Film Festival in France. Since then, three films directed by Apichatpong Weerasethakul have won recognition at Cannes: *Sud sanaeha* (*Blissfully Yours*) in 2002, *Sud*

Tears of the Black Tiger wowed audiences with its colorful sets and bloody plot.

pralad (*Tropical Malady*) in 2004, and *Loong Boonmee raleuk chat* (*Uncle Boonmee Who Can Recall His Past Lives*) in 2010. *Uncle Boonmee* won the Palme d'Or (Golden Palm), the prize for the best film in the festival.

Literature

Before the mid-1800s, Thai literature was written in verse. Its stories came from two main sources: Hindu religious classics and *Jataka Tales*, a collection of legends about the previous lives of the Buddha. All these works were written by and for the elite. Then, in the late nineteenth century, a number of well-known Chinese

Uncle Boonmee Who Can Recall His Past Lives concerns a man on his deathbed interacting with the spirits of his wife, son, and others from his past.

Chart Korbjitti published his first short novel in 1979, at age twenty-five. In the years since, he has produced many award-winning short stories and novels.

classics began to be translated into Thai, and the first modern works of Thai poetry, short stories, and novels appeared.

The most important Thai writer of this period was Sunthorn Phu (1787–1855), a court poet whose epic poem *Phra Aphaimani* (the name of the story's hero) is considered one of Thailand's greatest literary creations. Using plain language that any Thai could understand, Sunthorn Phu wrote affectingly about the lives and struggles of ordinary people. In the 1920s and 1930s, many Thai novelists wrote about social issues such as class and inequality. Siburapha's novel *Behind the Painting* (1937) deals with the lives of the elite and the difficulties of being a woman in Thai society. One of Thailand's most successful modern novelists is Chart Korbjitti. His works, such as *The End of the Road* (1980), deal with the difficulties faced by working-class Thais.

Sports and Games

Two traditional Thai sports are *muay Thai* and *takraw*. Often called Thailand's national sport, muay Thai is a martial art similar to kickboxing. Boxers use their feet, elbows, knees, and shoulders to best their opponents over three five-minute rounds. In traditional muay Thai, opponents must perform a ritual dance of respect before the bout begins, and a musical group performs during the match.

Takraw is a far gentler pastime, and a game that Thai children learn to play at a young age. There are many different versions of the game. *Sepak takraw* resembles volleyball. Under its rules, opponents try to keep a woven rattan ball from touching the ground on their side of a net without using their hands. Another form of the sport involves scoring through a hoop, as in basketball.

Kite flying is a traditional sport that is popular during the hot season in March and April, when rising air currents make for ideal flying conditions. During these months, kites of all sizes, colors, and shapes crowd the skies. Sometimes, skillful kite handlers participate in contests to knock each other's kites out of the air.

Western sports are also extremely popular in Thailand. All Thai children participate in school sports programs that include gymnastics, track and field, table tennis, badminton, and basketball. Soccer has become a national passion, and rugby and golf are becoming more popular.

A row of young men holds on to a large kite during a kite festival in central Thailand.

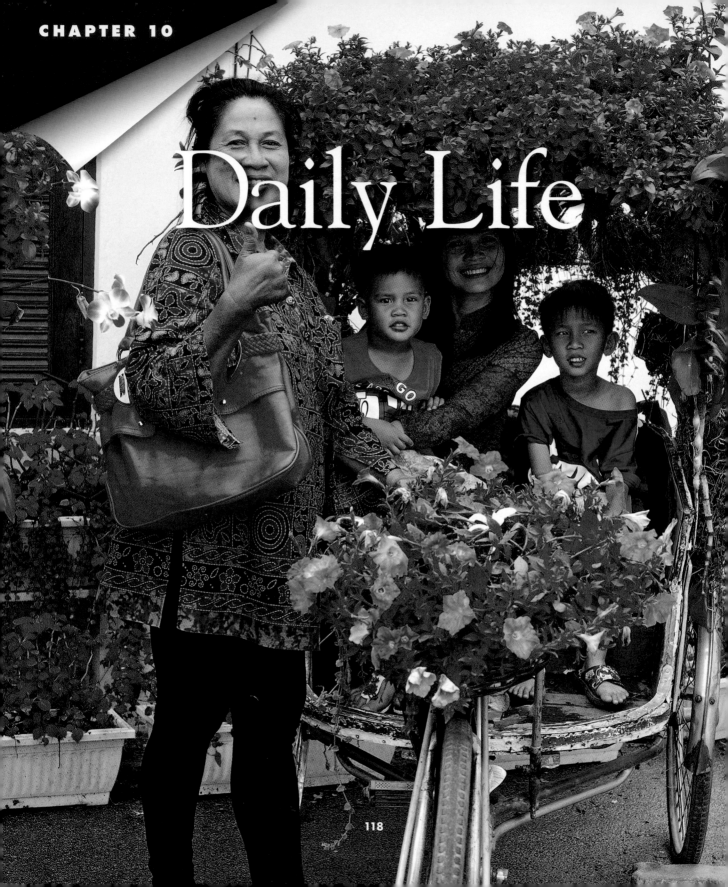

CHAPTER 10

Daily Life

IN THAILAND TODAY, TRADITION AND MODERNITY compete to shape everyday life. The force of tradition obliges Thais to preserve the customs and values that have guided families for generations. At the same time, the appeal of modernity—symbolized by smartphones and fast-paced urban lifestyles—is working to loosen the grip of the old ways and transform them into something new and different.

Opposite: **A family poses at a garden in Chiang Rai, in northern Thailand. Most Thai families have one or two children.**

Family Values

Very young children in Thailand are usually given great freedom. They are encouraged to play and are rarely disciplined. As they grow older, though, they are gradually given greater responsibilities. For example, they might be required to feed the animals, help raise crops, or look after their younger sisters or brothers. Sometimes, to supplement the family income, they are taught arts and crafts such as basket weaving, jewelry making, silk weaving, or embroidery.

Perhaps the most important message children learn is to respect their elders. In Thailand, one's elders are considered one's betters and therefore automatically worthy of obedience. Children are taught to obey their parents, grandparents, and even their older siblings. Fathers are the heads of families, but mothers, too, are entitled to respect. They manage the household and, in most cases, its financial affairs. Children know that they will be expected to care for their parents in their old age. They also know that they must honor their teachers. It would be unthinkable for a Thai student to challenge a teacher's judgment or correct a teacher's mistake.

The Wai

One way in which Thais show respect to one another is through a traditional gesture of the hands called a *wai*. Wais are greetings exchanged between two people of unequal rank. The younger or lower-ranking person always initiates the gesture, which is then returned by the higher-ranking person. You make a wai by pressing your palms gracefully together at chest level with your fingers pointing upward. As you do this, bow your head slightly until your face touches your hands.

Depending on the circumstances, a wai can mean "Hello," "Thank you," "Good-bye," or "I'm sorry." Most Thais today will try to save foreigners the embarrassment of making clumsy wais by shaking hands with them.

The Land of Smiles

In the Thai worldview, social harmony must be maintained, even at the expense of one's own feelings. Public displays of anger or unhappiness are traditionally rare among Thais. Instead, Thais have learned to smile in situations in which negative emotions might flare up. Everyone smiles in Thailand, no matter what a person might really be feeling inside. This national habit has earned Thailand the nickname "the land of smiles." By one count, Thais use thirteen different smiles in varying social circumstances.

Family Events

In the past, parents chose spouses for their children. Today, most Thai men and women are free to marry whomever they choose.

The traditional color for a bride's gown is pink. A groom may dress in a Western-style suit or in a high-necked Thai

Thai teenagers relax near a canal in Bangkok.

In Thai weddings, a white thread links the bride and groom, showing that their futures are intertwined.

jacket and trousers. As the couple kneels side by side, they are linked symbolically by a loop of white thread around their heads or wrists. Older people pour purified water on the bride's and groom's hands. There is no religious ceremony. Monks may be invited and give blessings, or the couple may go to a temple to make a donation for the occasion. Increasingly, young Thais are delaying marriage until after they complete their education.

What Year Is It in Thailand?

If you want to know what year it is in Thailand, just add 543 years to the current year in the Western calendar. The traditional Thai calendar dates time from the enlightenment of the Buddha, which by custom is said to have occurred in 543 BCE, as counted by the Western dating system. For day-to-day business and government affairs, Thailand follows the Western calendar.

As education among Thai women has improved, the number of children they are having has dropped. In 1970, Thai women had an average of 6 children; in 2012, that average was down to about 1.7.

Holidays and Festivals

Two of the most popular holidays are Songkran, which ushers in the Thai New Year, and Loi Krathong, an ancient festival of thanksgiving.

On Songkran, Thai families gather to symbolically wash away their sins from the previous year. It is a joyous event

During the northern Thai festival called Lanna, Thais release lanterns into the sky.

during which celebrants make merit by giving gifts to monks, paying respects to elders, and cleansing Buddha images with water. Because the holiday falls in April, typically the hottest month of the year, the cleansing ritual has, over time, turned into what has been called the world's largest water fight. Happy Thais, armed with water buckets, water pistols, and water cannons, douse each other and everything else in sight with lots and lots of water. It's all in good fun, and in some parts of the country, it goes on for days.

An elephant sprays water onto people during the Songkran festival.

Holidays in Thailand

New Year's Day	January 1
Makha Bucha	February
Chakri Day	April 6
Songkran (Thai New Year)	April 13–15
Labor Day	May 1
Coronation Day	May 5
Visakha Bucha	May
Royal Ploughing Ceremony	Early May
Asanha Bucha	July
Queen's Birthday	August 12
Chulalongkorn Day	October 23
Loi Krathong	November
King's Birthday	December 5
Constitution Day	December 10

Loi Krathong is another water-related holiday. On it, Thais honor the goddess who provides them with life-sustaining water. People create small floats, called *krathong*, from banana leaves and load them with flowers, incense, coins, and candles. Then they head down to the nearest river or lake to light the candles, make a wish, and set their floats adrift. According to legend, if your krathong floats out of view before its candle burns out, your wish will come true.

The Surin Elephant Roundup

One of the most spectacular local festivals in Thailand is the annual elephant roundup in northeastern Surin Province. The roundup, which takes place in November, features about one hundred elephants and their *mahouts*, or expert trainers and handlers.

Good to Eat

Thai cuisine is famous throughout the world. Among the common ingredients of dishes are garlic, chili peppers, lime juice, shrimp paste, coconut milk, lemongrass, and fish sauce.

Rice is the basic element of Thai cuisine. It is often served with spicy meat, vegetables, fish, seafood, or eggs. A favorite dish is pad Thai, a mix of stir-fried noodles and bits of dry or fresh shrimp that is sometimes topped with chopped peanuts. Noodle dishes, adapted from Chinese cuisine, are very popular.

The roundup features a number of events designed to showcase the grace, strength, and intelligence of elephants. Events include a tug-of-war between an elephant and about a hundred men, an elephant soccer match, an elephant race, and a reenactment of a classic battle involving elephant cavalry. The first public roundup was held in 1960.

Minding Your Manners in Thailand

Do not blow your nose in public.

Do not keep your shoes on when entering a home or a Buddhist temple.

Do not touch a Thai on the head. Buddhists believe that the head is the holiest part of the body, the location of the soul.

Do not sit with your feet pointing at anyone. Feet are believed to be the least holy part of the body.

Do not show disrespect in any way for the monarchy. If you drop a bill or a coin, do not step on it, because it bears the image of the king.

Modern Life

Thai society has undergone rapid change since the 1960s, when the country shifted to an industrial economy. Many people moved to the city in search of better jobs. As incomes rose in cities and villages, a new middle class emerged. Increasingly, houses were built of brick and concrete and equipped with electricity and modern plumbing. Thais had more money to spend on cars, televisions, and the latest phones and electronics. Villagers in the remotest areas no longer needed to be isolated from other Thais or the rest of the world. Better health care increased both the quality and the length of life that the average Thai could expect.

Today, in cities across the nation, people typically live in tall apartment buildings with stores or other businesses on the ground floor. Unlike the slow and predictable rhythms of village life, the beat of Thailand's urban areas is fast and frenzied. Bangkok sets the trends for the entire country in fashions and attitudes. Thai classical music and dance have increasingly given way to rock and roll and Western dance moves. For many urban residents, the wat and Buddhism are less relevant to their lives. As a result, wat attendance in cities has declined.

There is no doubt that Thailand faces new challenges in the twenty-first century. It must strike a balance between its most-revered traditions and the beneficial aspects of modernity. It must protect its natural resources and beautiful environment while expanding its economy to improve the living standards of its people. If any people can find answers to these perplexing problems, it is likely to be the gracious and tolerant Thais.

Timeline

People establish settlements in what is now northeastern Thailand.	ca. 3600 BCE
Mon and Khmer civilizations spread into parts of Thailand.	6th–9th centuries CE
Tai-speaking peoples begin migrating into what is now Thailand.	900s
Indraditya founds kingdom of Sukhothai.	Early 1200s
Sukhothai experiences a "Golden Age" under King Ramkhamhaeng.	1279–1298
The Ayutthaya kingdom is established.	1351
Portuguese become the first Europeans to reach Ayutthaya.	1511
Burmese troops destroy Ayutthaya; they are expelled by Taksin, who becomes king and moves the Thai capital to Thonburi.	1767
Taksin is killed; Chao Phraya Chakri founds the Chakri dynasty and moves the capital to Bangkok.	1782

WORLD HISTORY

ca. 2500 BCE	The Egyptians build the pyramids and the Sphinx in Giza.
ca. 563 BCE	The Buddha is born in India.
313 CE	The Roman emperor Constantine legalizes Christianity.
610	The Prophet Muhammad begins preaching a new religion called Islam.
1054	The Eastern (Orthodox) and Western (Roman Catholic) Churches break apart.
1095	The Crusades begin.
1215	King John seals the Magna Carta.
1300s	The Renaissance begins in Italy.
1347	The plague sweeps through Europe.
1453	Ottoman Turks capture Constantinople, conquering the Byzantine Empire.
1492	Columbus arrives in North America.
1500s	Reformers break away from the Catholic Church, and Protestantism is born.
1776	The U.S. Declaration of Independence is signed.
1789	The French Revolution begins.

THAI HISTORY

Rama III signs a treaty giving special trading rights to British merchants.	**1826**
Thailand enters World War I on the side of the Western Allies.	**1917**
Foreign-educated officials and army officers overthrow the absolute monarchy.	**1932**
Bhumibol Adulyadej becomes king.	**1946**
Thai forces fight on the side of U.S. forces in the Vietnam War.	**1960s–1970s**
Thailand's economy booms.	**Mid-1980s– mid-1990s**
Thailand suffers a severe economic downturn.	**1997**
A tsunami kills 8,000 people in Thailand.	**2004**
Military leaders oust Prime Minister Thaksin Shinawatra.	**2006**
Supporters and opponents of Thaksin stage mass protests during a period of political instability.	**2008–2010**
Yingluck Shinawatra becomes the country's first female prime minister.	**2011**
The Constitutional Court removes Prime Minister Yingluck Shinawatra from office; the military takes control of the government.	**2014**

WORLD HISTORY

1865	The American Civil War ends.
1879	The first practical lightbulb is invented.
1914	World War I begins.
1917	The Bolshevik Revolution brings communism to Russia.
1929	A worldwide economic depression begins.
1939	World War II begins.
1945	World War II ends.
1969	Humans land on the Moon.
1975	The Vietnam War ends.
1989	The Berlin Wall is torn down as communism crumbles in Eastern Europe.
1991	The Soviet Union breaks into separate states.
2001	Terrorists attack the World Trade Center in New York City and the Pentagon near Washington, D.C.
2004	A tsunami in the Indian Ocean destroys coastlines in Africa, India, and Southeast Asia.
2008	The United States elects its first African American president.

Fast Facts

Official name: Kingdom of Thailand

Capital: Bangkok

Official language: Thai

Bangkok

National flag

Phi Phi Islands

Official religion:	None
National anthem:	"Phleng Chat" ("National Song")
Government:	Constitutional monarchy
Head of state:	Monarch
Head of government:	Prime minister
Area of country:	198,117 square miles (513,120 sq km)
Geographic center:	15° N, 100° E
Bordering countries:	Myanmar to the north and west, Laos to the north and east, Cambodia to the southeast, and Malaysia to the south
Highest elevation:	Doi Inthanon, 8,481 feet (2,585 m)
Average high temperature:	In Bangkok, 97°F (36°C) in April; 91°F (33°C) in October
Average low temperature:	In Bangkok, 81°F (27°C) in April; 77°F (25°C) in October
Average annual rainfall:	In the north, 67 inches (170 cm); in the west, less than 40 inches (102 cm); in the south, 150 inches (381 cm)

Ayutthaya

Currency

**National population
(2012 est.):** 69.9 million

**Population of major
cities (2010 est.):**

Bangkok	8,280,925
Nonthaburi City	262,158
Pak Kret	178,114
Hat Yai	158,007
Nakhon Ratchasima	142,645
Chiang Mai	142,632

Landmarks:
- ▶ *Ayutthaya*, north of Bangkok
- ▶ *Damnoen Saduak Floating Market*, north of Bangkok
- ▶ *Khao Yai National Park*, Khorat
- ▶ *Phuket Island*, Malay Peninsula
- ▶ *Wat Phra Kaeo*, Bangkok

Economy: In 2012, the service sector contributed 44.2 percent of Thailand's gross domestic product; industry, 43.6 percent; and farming, 12.3 percent. Principal crops are rice, pineapples, shrimp, cashews, cassavas, vegetables, and flowers. Key manufactured goods include electronics, vehicles, machinery and equipment, and foodstuffs. Thailand is rich in natural resources, including tin, zinc, coal, limestone, and gypsum. Tourism contributes greatly to the national income. Each year, millions of tourists from around the world visit Thailand.

Currency: The baht. In 2014, 1 baht equaled US$0.031 and US$1.00 equaled 32 baht.

**System of weights
and measures:** The metric system, except for the measure of land, which uses traditional Thai measures.

**Literacy rate
(2005 est.):** 96%

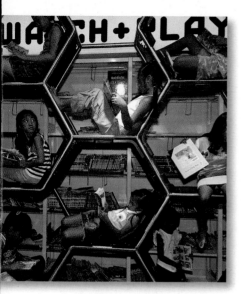

Children in a library

Bhumibol Adulyadej

Common Thai words and phrases:

Sabaai dii reu?	How are you?
Sabaai dii.	I'm fine.
Khor thoot.	Excuse me.
Khorp khun.	Thank you.
Khun chu arai?	What is your name?
Mai pen rai.	Never mind; it doesn't matter.
Aroi!	Delicious!

Prominent Thais:

Bhumibol Adulyadej (1927–)
King Rama IX

Chao Phraya Chakri (1737–1809)
Rama I, founder of the Chakri dynasty

Indraditya (?–ca. 1270)
Founder of Sukhothai

Sunthorn Phu (1787–1855)
Writer

Suriyothai (?–1548)
Ayutthaya queen and hero

Apichatpong Weerasethakul (1970–)
Filmmaker

Misiem Yipintsoi (1906–1988)
Artist

To Find Out More

Books

▶ Aloian, Molly. *Cultural Traditions of Thailand*. New York: Crabtree, 2013.

▶ Brennan, Francis. *Elephants*. New York: Children's Press, 2013.

▶ Ricker, Andy. *Pok Pok: Food and Stories from the Streets, Homes, and Roadside Restaurants of Thailand*. Berkeley: Ten Speed Press, 2013.

Music

▶ *Royal Court Music of Thailand*. Washington, DC: Smithsonian/ Folkways, 1994.

▶ *Thailand*. London, UK: World Music Network, 2003.

▶ Visit this Scholastic Web site for more information on Thailand:
www.factsfornow.scholastic.com
Enter the keyword **Thailand**

Index

Page numbers in *italics*
indicate illustrations.

trade, 30, 47, 48, 52, 54, 55, 60, 77–78, 79, 110
transportation, *22*, 32, 81, 102
Tropical Malady (film), 113–114
tropical rain forests, 30, 33–34
tsunamis, 24, *24*

U

Uncle Boonmee Who Can Recall His Past Lives (film), 114, *114*
United States, 52, 58, 59–60, *60*

V

Vajiravudh (king), 56, *56*, 109
Vietnam War, 59
villages. *See also* cities; towns.
    Akha people, 90, *90*
    gates to, 90, *90*
    governments of, 74
    silk industry in, 111
    subdistricts and, 74
    Thonburi as, 49
Visakha Bucha holiday, 102

W

wai (greetings), 120, *120*
Wang River, 17
Wat Arun, 51–52, 75
Wat Chiang Man, 22, *44*
water buffalo, 31, *31*
Wat Pho, 75
Wat Phra Kaeo, 51, 100, *100*, *108*
Wat Saket, 8
weaving, *111*
Weerasethakul, Apichatpong, 113–114, 133
weights and measures, 81
white elephants, 32, 67, *67*, 74
wildflowers, *14*
wildlife. *See* amphibian life; animal life; insect life; marine life; plant life; reptilian life.
women. *See also* people.

Akha, 90–91
childbirth, 123
clothing, 90–91
craftwork of, 89
education of, 92
Hmong, 89, *89*
marriage, 121
monarchs as, 65
neck coils, 91, *91*
nuns, 101–102
Padaung, 91, *91*
silk production and, 111
as village heads, 74
voting rights, *69*
World War II, 58

Y

Yawi language, 87
Yipintsoi, Misiem, 108, 133
Yom River, 17

Meet the Author

MEL FRIEDMAN IS AN AWARD-WINNING JOURNALIST and children's book author. As a journalist, he has written articles on the media, civil liberties, nuclear weapons, and health. He has also worked as an editorial consultant for the United Nations. He is the author of children's books on China, Iraq, Australia, Antarctica, Africa, the city of Istanbul, the samurai of Japan, and the 1929 stock market crash. In 1992, an article Friedman wrote on media coverage of nuclear weapons issues won a Lowell Mellett Award from the Penn State University School of Communications.

Friedman holds a degree in history from Lafayette College in Pennsylvania. He also did graduate work at Columbia University in political science and international affairs with a focus on East Asia. He holds four graduate degrees from Columbia, where he learned to speak and read Chinese.

Friedman and his wife, who is also a writer, live in New York City. They have a daughter, and occasionally take in—or find homes for—stray dogs.

Photo Credits